THE BRITISH TV DETECTIVE & ESPIONAGE CASEBOOK

THE BRITISH TV DETECTIVE & ESPIONAGE CASEBOOK

HOW BRITISH TELEVISION BUILT THE ANATOMY OF INVESTIGATION

PAUL BISHOP

The British TV Detective & Espionage Casebook

ISBN: 979-8-9953571-3-1

Printed in the United States of America

DEDICATION

For Dell
For each and every reason...

ACKNOWLEDGEMENTS

Thanks as always to the usual suspects...
Lysander Fox, Claudia Sherwood, Jenna Winston,
Ivy Andrews, and Atticus Imp
For service above and beyond.

TABLE OF CONTENTS

PART THREE—THE LITERARY DETECTIVES

PART FOUR—THE MODERN ERA

PART FIVE—THE AMATEURS & ODDBALLS

AUTHOR'S NOTE

HOW BRITISH TV GOT IT RIGHT

I was born in England and grew up watching British television. When I was eight years old, my family immigrated to the United States, and I continued growing up in the hot-rod and surfing culture of California. During the 1970s, when a handful of British mystery shows occasionally appeared on our local Public Broadcasting Station, I found myself drawn back to police dramas coming out of the UK. Even then, as a teenager, I noticed they were different from American shows. They moved differently. They talked differently. The police officers felt like working people rather than television heroes. At that point I was still more English than American, and those shows were a connection to something I had not entirely left behind.

What is difficult to explain now, in the age of streaming, is how hard these shows were to find. During the 1970s, 1980s, and well into the 1990s, British television was not readily available in the United States. There was no BritBox, no Acorn TV, no YouTube, and even British programs appearing on PBS were sporadic, often scheduled at odd hours, with no guarantee you would ever see the full series. If you missed an episode, you missed it.

To watch the British cop shows I cared about, I relied on bootleg VHS tapes sent over from England to a specialty shop carrying British goods. The owner's family would record programs from their television, mail the tapes to the store, and the shop would rent them out for a couple of dollars a night to those of us who kept coming back for more. It felt like an underground version of Blockbuster. If you wanted to follow a series, you put your name on a list, waited for the tape to arrive, rented it for a night or two, and hoped the tracking held long enough to make it all the way through.

I also fanatically collected tie-in novels associated with my favorite shows, but tracking down those connected to British television required the same persistence as viewing the programs themselves. This was all pre-Internet. If you wanted British TV tie-in books, you wrote letters, searched used bookstores, called specialty shops, and asked other fans if they knew where a copy could be found. Locating British television shows and the books connected to them became an effort in itself.

As the years passed, I became more American. I became a citizen and built a life and career in my adopted country. In some ways, though, I remained British, and my fondness for British food, books, and television never left me. I eventually joined the Los Angeles Police Department and spent thirty-five years on the job, working a variety of assignments, including more than two decades specializing in sexual assault investigations and later supervising a unit of thirty detectives. I spent a great deal of that time in interview rooms, squad rooms, and in the long, deliberate process of building cases. I later taught interrogation techniques to law enforcement officers across the country. In other words, I spent most of my adult life inside real investigations. Through all those years, I kept watching British police shows.

As my career progressed, something became increasingly clear. British television seemed to understand aspects of the job American television often overlooked. Earlier American police shows were built around action, car chases, gunfights, and clearly defined heroes and villains. They were designed to move quickly and entertain. British series took a different approach. They moved more deliberately. Detectives talked to people. They made mistakes. They argued with supervisors. They completed reports. They worried about promotions. They drank too much, went home too late, and returned to work the next morning to start again. Cases did not always resolve cleanly. American cop shows made the job seem all action and fun, but British police dramas showed it as requiring dedication and hard work, which I knew to be closer to the truth.

Over time, another pattern emerged. If you watched enough British detective series and paid attention to what detectives were actually doing, a structure began to appear. You could see the difference between uniform and CID. You could see how a major case was organized. You could see the role of the interview, the role of informants, the role of forensic evidence, the role of supervision, and the role of internal politics. You could watch the job evolve, from the village bobby to the Flying Squad, from the lone detective to the incident room, from the interview room to the forensic lab, from the individual investigator to the investigative team.

Across decades, British television created something close to a working model of investigative practice. Not perfect, of course. Television remains television. Taken as a whole, these series presented the job from multiple angles: the street, the interview room, the squad room, the command office, and eventually the forensic lab and the major incident team. They showed policing as a career, as a way of thinking, and ultimately as a system.

This book grew out of that recognition. It is not a guide to television programs, and it is not a nostalgic look at past series. It examines British television detective and espionage dramas as case studies in how investigation works. The spies show how information is gathered and used. The working detectives show how policing functions as a profession. The literary detectives show how intellect, education, and personality shape how crimes are solved. The modern detectives show how investigations are conducted as large, coordinated systems. And the amateurs and outsiders show that sometimes the person who solves the crime is the one who sees the world differently.

I spent my career conducting interviews, running investigations, and supervising detectives. I spent my evenings, when I was not called out to a crime scene, watching British detective series. Somewhere along the way, I realized I was not simply watching television. I was watching a profession being portrayed, one series, one detective, and one case at a time. This book is about that profession.

Paul Bishop
Somewhere North of Los Angeles
2027

INTRODUCTION

OPENING THE CASE

This book is not a guide to television programs. It is a study of a profession.

The British TV Detective & Espionage Casebook explores how British television has portrayed those who investigate crime and conduct intelligence work, and what those portrayals reveal about the work itself. The series discussed here matter not simply because they were popular or long-running, but because each captures a distinct aspect of the investigative world. Considered individually, they are compelling dramas. Viewed together, they form something more substantial, a working map of investigation, an anatomy of how the job is imagined, structured, and carried out over time.

British television approaches investigators differently from its American counterparts. American series tend to emphasize the case, the pace, or the resolution in court. The structure often moves forward through action and outcome. British series, by contrast, place the investigator at the center of the narrative. The interest lies not only in what happened, but in who is trying to understand it. Attention is given to background, education, temperament, and the environment in which the investigator operates. The job is shaped as much by these factors as by the crime itself.

Rank matters. Class matters. Education matters. Personality matters. A constable on patrol sees the world differently from a chief inspector directing a major inquiry. A detective working in a rural village approaches a case differently from one operating in a large city. An intelligence officer evaluates information differently from a police officer building evidence. Each position carries its own assumptions, limitations, and advantages. Even within the same organization, perspective shifts with experience and responsibility.

The amateur investigator disrupts this structure. Operating outside formal systems, the amateur is not bound by procedure or hierarchy. That absence can be a disadvantage, limiting access and authority, but it can also create freedom. Without training directing attention in specific ways, the amateur may notice what the professional overlooks. British television returns to this figure repeatedly, suggesting insight is not confined to those who hold official positions.

The book is built on a direct premise. There is no single way to investigate anything. There are different kinds of investigators, different institutional frameworks, and different ways of thinking about the same problem. British television, across several decades, has managed to portray nearly all of them, sometimes deliberately, sometimes as a byproduct of strong storytelling. The structure of this book follows five of those approaches, each representing a distinct method of engaging with the task of bringing transparency to what has happened.

The first is Secrets, the world of intelligence officers, informants, handlers, and quiet conflicts conducted out of public view. This is the domain of espionage, where information carries greater weight than evidence, where ambiguity is constant, and where success is often defined by events that never occur.

The second is Profession, the world of the working police officer, from the uniform constable to the senior investigating officer. This is the domain of patrol cars, interview rooms, paperwork, and the steady construction of a case that must withstand legal scrutiny. It is structured, procedural, and often slow, shaped by rules designed to ensure the result holds.

The third is Mind, the domain of the intellectual and literary detective, where observation, education, and a recognition of human behavior take precedence. These figures often stand slightly apart from formal systems, not entirely outside them, but not fully defined by them. Their authority comes from how they think.

The fourth is Method, the modern investigative landscape shaped by forensic science, media attention, legal oversight, and complex, large-scale inquiries. Here, the detective operates within an expanded system including laboratories, databases, legal review, and public pressure. The work becomes collaborative, technical, and increasingly visible.

The fifth is Perspective, the world of the outsider and the amateur, individuals who investigate not because it is their profession, but because of how they see the world. These include priests, scholars, retirees, eccentrics, and others whose value lies in their distance from established practice.

Each section isolates a distinct approach, grouping television series that exemplify a particular way of working. The focus is not on summarizing plots or cataloguing episodes, but on what these series reveal about the work itself. How are decisions made when information is incomplete? How do investigators determine what matters and what does not? How does bureaucracy shape the course of an inquiry? What role does experience play in recognizing patterns? What happens when personal involvement alters judgment? And how does the work change when the investigator operates without formal authority?

These portrayals form a pattern. The distinctions between different kinds of investigators are real, but not absolute. The spy and the detective, at first glance very different, confront many of the same problems. Both gather information. Both assess credibility. Both operate in environments where certainty is difficult to achieve. The uniform constable and the senior investigator perform different functions, yet remain part of the same structure, each dependent on the other for the process to work.

The amateur often succeeds for the same reasons as the professional. Attention, patience, and human behavior insights are not exclusive to training. They are habits of mind. Whether the investigator carries official authority or not, the essential task remains the same, to understand what has happened and why.

Investigation depends less on authority than on mindset. It rests on the ability to notice what others overlook, to recognize when an explanation does not hold, and to stay with a problem long enough for its structure to reveal itself. It requires patience, persistence, and a willingness to reconsider assumptions. It also involves repetition, routine, and, more often than not, paperwork.

British television, perhaps without intending to do so, has produced one of the most complete portraits of investigative work in popular culture. From the constable on night patrol to the intelligence officer working quietly behind a desk, from the country house amateur to the modern detective surrounded by data and scrutiny, these series show not only how crimes and conspiracies are resolved, but how the people responsible for resolving them think, work, and live.

This is the subject of this book. Not television as entertainment, but television as a lens through which to examine the people and professions involved in finding the truth, and the many different ways the task can be approached.

PART ONE

THE QUIET PROFESSIONALS

Covering the intelligence side of investigations. The people who build files, recruit informants, run operations, and make decisions destined never to appear in court records.

INTRODUCTION—THE SECRET WAR

The British TV Detective & Espionage Casebook begins with a simple premise. Investigation, in all its forms, follows a shared logic.

On British television, the police detective and the intelligence officer are not opposites. They operate in parallel. One works the streets. The other moves in the shadows. Both deal in information, motive, and truth. One builds a criminal case. The other assembles an intelligence file. Both conduct interviews, cultivate informants, and recognize deception, fear, and hesitation. Both spend long hours in reports, waiting for the detail that brings everything else into focus. In practice, the spy is a detective working under different rules, and with greater consequences.

The parallel is not always immediately apparent. The detective operates within a visible system. The intelligence officer works within one deliberately obscured from view. Evidence, in police work, is meant to be presented. Intelligence is often protected, withheld, or used without acknowledgment. Beneath those differences lies a shared discipline. Both must decide what matters, what can be trusted, and what conclusions can be drawn from incomplete information.

Espionage stands at the outset of this casebook. Before the uniformed constable, the Flying Squad, provincial CID, and the literary detective, the parallel system shaping investigative work must be understood. It operates largely out of sight, where individuals rarely step forward and outcomes seldom appear in public record. The methods remain familiar. Authority differs, and the consequences follow from it.

British espionage drama has rarely been concerned with spectacle. Gadgets, explosions, and grand declarations belong elsewhere. From the 1960s onward, the emphasis has been on the work itself. Surveillance, reports, waiting, compromise, and the gradual erosion from carrying out tasks that cannot be openly acknowledged. The lasting appeal of these series lies in attention to process, to the accumulation of small decisions eventually shaping larger outcomes.

The section proceeds from a simple premise. Espionage is not a single role, but a collection of roles functioning within a system. Each series represents a different position inside that structure. Together they form a composite view of the intelligence world as imagined by British television across decades. No one figure defines the work. Interaction between them creates the full picture.

At one end stands the field professional. In *Danger Man*, John Drake operates as an investigator, meeting contacts, testing information, and determining what can be trusted. His work resembles that of a detective, but is carried out on an international stage, where jurisdiction is fluid and accountability less certain.

Behind him sits the structure supporting the field. *The Rat Catchers* shifts attention to offices, briefings, files, and internal maneuvering. The focus moves away from the individual and toward the machinery directing him. Espionage begins to resemble administration, and the system itself becomes central to the decision making process.

A part of the work remains unspoken. If the system exists and threats are real, someone must handle what cannot be formalized.

Callan occupies that space. This is not the professional operating within clear boundaries, but the operative dealing with informants, coercion, and decisions carrying lasting weight. If *Danger Man* presents how the job is meant to function, *Callan* reveals the cost when it does not.

Such work does not occur without direction. Authority sits elsewhere. In *The Sandbaggers*, attention turns to the controller, the figure assigning risk and absorbing consequence. Meetings replace movement, and decisions are shaped by politics as much as necessity. Any remaining sense of glamour gives way to responsibility and constraint.

As time passes, the environment changes. The Cold War recedes, new threats emerge, and intelligence work accelerates. *Spooks* presents a modern section operating as a coordinated unit. Analysts, field officers, and technical specialists work under constant pressure, where success often goes unnoticed and failure is immediate.

Above the operational level sits the strategist. In the adaptations of John le Carré, most notably *Smiley's People*, espionage unfolds as a long-term investigation. George Smiley proceeds through patience and analysis, assembling his position over time rather than acting in the moment. The work resembles detection at its most deliberate, where progress depends on interpretation rather than action.

Not every situation can be resolved through patience. Some require direct intervention. *The Professionals* represents that function, where enforcement replaces subtlety and decisions are carried out without delay. It serves as a reminder behind planning and preparation lies the moment when force is applied.

A few fall outside the system. Every intelligence service produces them. In *Man in a Suitcase*, McGill moves through the margins, a former agent no longer connected to the organization but unable to separate himself from its world. Experience remains, even when affiliation does not.

At the far edge are those who remain within the system but without purpose. *Slow Horses* presents Slough House as the destination for those sidelined. They are not dismissed, but neither are they trusted. Their presence reflects a system retaining what it cannot fully discard, and the quiet acknowledgment failure is part of its design.

These series construct a portrait of a profession through its parts. The field operative, the bureaucracy, the enforcer, the strategist, the team, the outsider, and the discarded all contribute to a larger structure. Each role carries its own pressures and isolation, yet none exists independently of the others. The system holds them together, even as it separates them.

This is the intelligence world British television presents. Not as spectacle, but as structure. Not as an individual pursuit, but as a system built on information, interpretation, and consequence. It shares that foundation with every police station and detective's office that follows in this Casebook.

It begins with a file.

DANGER MAN—THE PROFESSIONAL

Before British television espionage became cynical, bureaucratic, and morally compromised, it was defined by professionalism. *Danger Man*, known in the United States as *Secret Agent*, established that tone from the outset. First appearing in 1960 and returning in a longer format in 1964, the show starred Patrick McGoohan as John Drake, a government agent sent across the world to deal with intelligence problems, political instability, and threats to national security. While often grouped with the spy boom of the 1960s, the show stands apart. James Bond is fantasy. John Drake is an employee.

Drake does not swagger into casinos in a tuxedo. He avoids gadgets and gimmicks, does not seduce women as part of the job, and in many episodes does not even carry a gun. None of this is accidental. McGoohan was specific about how the character should be portrayed, insisting Drake would not be a womanizer and would avoid firearms whenever possible. The result is a character defined by intelligence, discipline, and restraint, a man who solves problems through patience, planning, and nerve rather than force. That choice, more than anything else, shaped the tone of British television espionage for years to come.

The work depicted is neither glamorous nor particularly exciting. It unfolds in hotel rooms, offices, and anonymous streets in foreign cities. Drake spends much of his time interviewing sources, verifying information, waiting for contacts, and adapting when operations begin to unravel. The cases involve political instability, defectors, missing scientists, and threats requiring containment before becoming public. His role is not to save the world, but to prevent problems from escalating. He operates with a clear realization every action carries consequences, and professionalism requires solving one problem without creating another.

Within British espionage drama, Drake represents the field professional. He is neither policymaker nor executioner, but the operative sent to handle situations quietly and efficiently. Preparation, observation, and controlled action define his approach. When the assignment is complete, he moves on without recognition or celebration. The discipline of the character, and of the narrative, would influence much of what followed.

The portrayal avoids both cynicism and naivety. Drake believes in the work, yet recognizes the world he operates in is shaped by compromise and uncertainty. He is not a blunt instrument like Callan, nor a strategist like George Smiley. His role is more immediate. He goes where he is sent and carries out the assignment as cleanly as circumstances allow. The idea of *clean* runs through the concept. The storytelling is direct. The visual style is restrained. Drake's methods emphasize control and efficiency. He prefers to outthink opponents rather than confront them physically. When violence occurs, it is brief and rarely satisfying. There is little of the stylized action found in other spy dramas of the period. Violence is treated as risk, not spectacle.

Equally important is Drake's place within an organization. He receives assignments, reports back, and operates within a defined chain of command. He is not a lone figure acting independently, but part of a larger structure. That distinction becomes increasingly significant across British espionage drama, where emphasis returns to authority, hierarchy, and decisions made away from the field. Operatives carry out the work, but do not originate it.

The show occupies a point just before the genre begins to darken. Drake still believes in the purpose of his work, even as the stories acknowledge outcomes are not always clear-cut. Some operations fail. Some individuals cannot be saved. Success is often partial, and at times it carries a cost. This underlying realism separates the concept from more flamboyant interpretations of espionage.

McGoohan's performance anchors the tone. His portrayal of Drake is controlled and observant, a man who listens carefully and acts with deliberation. There is little excess in the character, and very little wasted movement. The intensity remains contained rather than displayed, reinforcing the idea of a professional who understands both the demands and the risks of the job.

An often overlooked aspect of *Danger Man* is the line of paperback tie-in novels published between 1962 and 1966. Six original titles—*Target for Tonight* by Richard Telfair, *Departure Deferred* and *Storm Over Rockall* by W. Howard Baker, *Hell for Tomorrow* by Peter Leslie, *The Exterminator* by W. A. Ballinger, and *No Way Out* by Wilfred McNeilly—extended Drake's world beyond the screen. In the United Kingdom they appeared under the *Danger Man* title, while in the United States they were released by Macfadden-Bartell as *Secret Agent*. These were original stories rather than adaptations, placing Drake in new assignments.

The novels often adopt a darker tone, particularly *Target for Tonight*, which presents Drake's early NATO work in the first person and offers a deeper sense of his background. Later titles align more closely with the hour-long format, where Drake operates for M9. Although multiple author names appear, several books were written by Arthur Athwill William Baker under different pseudonyms. Across these stories, the emphasis remains consistent. Drake is a professional intelligence officer, operating in a harsher and more dangerous world than television at the time could fully depict.

Danger Man establishes espionage as a profession defined by discipline, restraint, and responsibility. Drake is not an adventurer or a symbol, but a trained operative working within limits he does not control, sent where he is needed and expected to complete the task without drawing attention.

The work in the field, however, is only part of the process. Every assignment begins elsewhere, shaped by those who gather information, assess risk, and decide where the operative will be sent. The structure exists before the agent arrives, and it continues long after he leaves.

THE RAT CATCHERS—THE SYSTEM

Espionage is rarely glamorous, and British television was quick to recognize it. At the height of the 1960s spy boom, when polished agents and international intrigue dominated popular culture, *The Rat Catchers* offered something far less appealing and far more grounded. Intelligence work here is not adventure. It is containment. Threats remain quiet, responses controlled, and the tone suggests a job closer to maintenance than heroism. The work matters, but is not meant to be visible.

Broadcast on ITV between 1966 and 1967, the show ran for two seasons and twenty-five hour-long episodes. Some stories unfolded across multiple installments with cliffhanger endings, giving the narrative a sense of continuity and consequence many programs of the period lacked. The tone remained sober and often bleak, more concerned with class tensions, moral compromise, and political reality than with gadgets or seduction. *The Rat Catchers* occupies a transitional point, bridging the romantic espionage of the early 1960s and the more cynical dramas that would follow.

At its center is a small, highly secret British intelligence unit tasked with addressing the most serious threats to national security. Known unofficially as the Rat Catchers, the group operates without public acknowledgment and answers directly to the Prime Minister. Their existence can be denied, their actions disavowed.

They are expected to succeed without recognition and to fail without consequence to those above them. They are not the men who pull the trigger. They determine where the gun will be pointed, and whether it will be used at all.

Within British espionage drama, the Rat Catchers represent the structure itself. They gather information, assess risk, and decide what action is required. Field agents may travel, fight, and occasionally die, but decisions originate elsewhere. Men like the Rat Catchers determine which problems justify that risk. They are the quiet mechanism behind the professional, the point at which intelligence becomes policy and policy becomes action.

The unit is composed of three men, each representing a different perspective on intelligence work. Peregrine Smith, played by Gerald Flood, is an Oxford-educated executive and managing director of Trans World Electronics, the corporation serving as the team's cover. He moves comfortably in upper-class and international environments, presenting himself as a charming, slightly frivolous businessman. Beneath that surface lies a capable operative, able to act decisively when required and to navigate situations demanding both diplomacy and force.

Brigadier Davidson, played by Philip Stone, serves as the unit's commanding officer and strategist. A former military man, he is controlled, analytical, and demanding. Working from a sparse office on the edge of Whitehall, he reveals little of himself and expects results from those around him. His authority is rarely questioned, yet he is aware intelligence work requires initiative. His relationship with Smith reflects that balance, discipline tempered by a degree of autonomy.

The third member of the unit is Scotland Yard Superintendent Richard Hurst, played by Glyn Owen. Hurst brings a different set of values, rooted in law enforcement. He believes in arrest, trial, and due process. His presence introduces constant tension. The Rat

Catchers operate in a world where those principles cannot always be applied. Brought into the unit for his investigative ability, Hurst must navigate a structure in which legality and necessity do not always align. His struggle to reconcile those differences provides much of the emotional weight.

The group's official cover, Trans World Electronics, allows Smith and Hurst to travel internationally and move through corporate and governmental environments without drawing attention. Davidson, notably, rarely leaves his office and holds no formal position within the company, reinforcing his role as a figure who exists almost entirely within the intelligence structure. He does not pursue suspects or conduct surveillance. He reads, evaluates, and decides. His authority is exercised through judgment rather than action.

Unlike many contemporary spy series, *The Rat Catchers* does not rely on elaborate action or extensive location work. Budget limitations confined much of the production to interior sets, with exterior sequences often limited to brief transitional shots. Despite this, the show maintains an international scope. Episodes take Smith and Hurst to locations such as Greece, Ireland, Madrid, Lisbon, and Stockholm, offering a sense of movement beyond the confines of the set. The emphasis, however, remains on decisions made in offices rather than actions carried out in the field.

Unfortunately, almost all the episodes of *The Rat Catchers* have been lost. When Associated Rediffusion lost its ITV franchise in 1968 and the industry moved toward color broadcasting, many black-and-white recordings were wiped or destroyed. Only a small number of episodes survive, often in poor-quality prints. Like many productions of the era, the series exists more in documentation and recollection than in accessible form, adding to its reputation as a lost piece of British television history.

The show also produced two tie-in novels, *All in a Day's Work* and *The End of the Fourth Reich*, written under the name David Ray. These were original stories rather than adaptations, extending the world of the series beyond the screen. The tone remains consistent with the television version, though at times darker, particularly in its depiction of the consequences of intelligence decisions. As with many tie-in works of the period, the novels explore areas television could not fully address, offering a more direct view of the moral cost attached to the work.

The Rat Catchers shifts attention away from the field and toward the machinery supporting it. Intelligence is gathered, organized, and evaluated in a world where success is rarely visible and seldom acknowledged. The work proceeds through analysis, discussion, and decision-making, each stage building toward an outcome that may never be publicly recognized.

Files accumulate, judgments form, and decisions take shape over time. Eventually, those decisions move beyond observation and into action, passing from those who study the problem to those expected to resolve it.

CALLAN—THE ASSASSIN

Intelligence work reaches a point where information is no longer enough. Files are built, surveillance completed, and decisions made. What follows is action. *Callan* enters at that moment. By the mid-1960s, British television had already begun moving away from fantasy toward a colder, more grounded portrayal of espionage. In that world, David Callan is the man sent to carry out what others have decided must be done.

In the late 1960s, *The Man From U.N.C.L.E.*, *Mission: Impossible*, *I Spy*, and *The Wild Wild West* rode the crest of the James Bond–inspired spy boom on American television. Across the Atlantic, espionage also dominated British screens, but the tone differed sharply.

While 007 remained the quintessential British spy, American television followed his lead most closely. On American TV, espionage was entertainment. There were gadgets, elaborate plots, flamboyant villains, and heroes who triumphed in style. The tone was energetic, colorful, and reassuring.

British television took a different path. Espionage was presented as work, and dangerous work at that. It was harsh, morally ambiguous, and frequently bleak. These spies were the opposite of Bond. If Bond represented fantasy, they suggested something closer to reality, where the job involved paperwork, betrayal, and violence carried out quietly and denied publicly.

In 1967, the British television drama *A Magnum for Schneider* introduced David Callan, a terse, controlled, and often pitiless operative who quickly became a defining figure in British espionage drama. The play's success led to *Callan*, which ran from 1967 to 1972 and remains one of the most uncompromising portrayals of intelligence work ever produced.

Callan works for a shadowy government agency known simply as The Section, responsible for internal security and counter-espionage. The organization operates with near-total autonomy and minimal oversight, and its methods are severe. Torture is used as an interrogation tool. Assassination is routine policy. Targets are placed in color-coded files, and when a file turns red, death follows. Few Western intelligence agencies have been depicted in such stark terms. Callan is the instrument used when quiet execution is required, controlled by a bureaucrat known only as Hunter, a man he both despises and cannot escape.

Within British espionage drama, Callan represents the assassin. He is not the one who gathers intelligence or determines policy. He receives the file after decisions have already been made. His role is not to investigate or debate, but to act. He stands at the point where paperwork becomes violence.

Created by James Mitchell and portrayed with controlled intensity by Edward Woodward, the character became the definitive anti-Bond. There is no glamour attached to the work. Callan is a tradesman of violence, a professional whose occupation happens to be killing. He approaches espionage as a job, one he often regrets but cannot abandon. His skill makes him valuable, while the nature of that skill ensures he is always expendable.

Isolation defines the character. Callan has no real allies. The closest approximation is Lonely, a disheveled, malodorous petty thief who exists on the margins of both society and the intelligence world. Their relationship is built on fear, money, and necessity, yet it carries an uneasy loyalty. They understand one another in ways others cannot. Both are damaged, both are trapped, and both continue because there are few alternatives.

Mitchell also expanded the character in prose. Several novels, beginning with *A Magnum for Schneider* (also published as *A Red File for Callan*), extended the story beyond television with original material. Titles such as *Russian Roulette* and *Death and Bright Water* place Callan in increasingly isolated situations, often emphasizing the psychological cost of the work. The tone is darker, exploring consequences television could only suggest.

A 1974 feature film, *Callan*, again based on *A Magnum for Schneider*, brought the character to the screen in a more concentrated form, with Woodward reprising the role. The film reinforces a central truth. Callan does not act out of ideology. He acts because he is instructed to, and because the work has become the structure of his life.

Additional short stories, later collected as *Callan Uncovered* and *Callan Uncovered 2*, further distill the character. The prose is direct and unadorned, mirroring the world in which Callan operates.

Callan helped define the darker, more realistic direction of British espionage drama. It removed any remaining sense of fantasy and replaced it with something more unsettling. There are no gadgets to resolve the situation, no elaborate villains, and very little sense of triumph. The work consists of pressure, compromise, and the knowledge that when decisions reach their final stage, someone like Callan will be sent to carry them out.

Callan operates at the point where decisions are executed. His role is direct, final, and often irreversible.

Responsibility, however, lies elsewhere. It belongs to those who decide which names are marked and which operations proceed. Callan is the instrument. Authority remains above him.

THE SANDBAGGERS—THE CONTROLLER

Most consequential decisions in intelligence work are made in rooms where nothing appears to happen. Conversations are measured, voices controlled, and the outcome of an operation may hinge on a single word. *The Sandbaggers* places its focus there, in the offices where orders are shaped, revised, and sometimes contested. It is a series about responsibility, the weight of authority, and the pressure that builds when decisions cannot be undone.

Premiering a decade after *Callan*, *The Sandbaggers* established a new standard for British espionage drama in the late 1970s. Created by Ian Mackintosh, it starred Roy Marsden as Neil Burnside, the hard-driving Deputy Director of Operations for the British Secret Intelligence Service. This was well before Marsden became widely associated with Adam Dalgliesh, and his performance here remains one of the most precise portrayals of intelligence leadership brought to television.

Running from 1978 to 1980, *The Sandbaggers* is grounded in procedure, compromise, and the quiet brutality of the intelligence world. There are no gadgets, no elaborate villain headquarters, and no theatrical displays of power. Only one explosion occurs in the entire series, and it comes in the opening episode. The drama instead builds through tension, moral compromise, and constant political maneuvering. It is a world of glances, pauses, and carefully chosen words, where decisions made in small offices carry consequences in distant places.

Mackintosh's background as a career naval officer contributed directly to the tone of the episodes. He aimed to present espionage as it is practiced rather than as it is imagined. His reading of intelligence structures and institutional rivalries gave the show an authenticity that raised concerns within government circles, leading to scripts being reviewed for security clearance prior to production. One episode was reportedly rejected altogether for being too close to real-world operations.

Within British espionage drama, Neil Burnside represents the controller. He does not gather intelligence in the field, nor carry out the final act. He reads reports, evaluates risk, argues with ministers, challenges rival departments, and ultimately decides whether an operation will proceed. His responsibility is not to act, but to determine when others will.

At the center stands Burnside, a man operating in a state of controlled intensity. He is intelligent, relentless, and wholly committed to protecting his section and completing his objectives. He is also simultaneously capable of ruthless decisions, sacrificing careers, reputations, and, when necessary, lives. His work is divided between managing operations and navigating bureaucracy, and often the greater danger comes from within his own organization rather than from foreign adversaries.

His primary resource is the Special Operations Section, known as the Sandbaggers, a term describing individuals who conceal their capabilities in order to gain advantage. Burnside rarely has more than a handful of operatives at his disposal, and often fewer. Agents are lost, compromised, or rendered unusable, and replacements are difficult to prepare and harder still to trust. This scarcity forces constant calculation, requiring Burnside to weigh national interest against the cost in human lives.

Among those who populate his world are Willy Caine, the most dependable of the Sandbaggers and a man uncomfortable with both firearms and questionable assignments; Diane Lawler, the logistics officer whose understated humor offsets the severity of the work; and Jeff Ross, the CIA station chief in London and Burnside's most consistent ally. Set against them are Burnside's own superiors and political overseers, including the head of SIS, known only as C, the suspicious Deputy Director Matthew Peele, and Sir Geoffrey Wellingham, Burnside's former father-in-law, whose loyalties shift with political necessity.

The conflicts within *The Sandbaggers* resist simple resolution. Burnside is frequently forced to act on incomplete or unreliable information. Plans are debated by officials whose priorities do not always align with operational reality. Miscommunication, misinformation, and betrayal shape outcomes as much as strategy. Success is often partial, and failure is sometimes unavoidable. Agents are lost, intelligence is compromised, and consequences ripple outward beyond immediate control.

Broadcast during the height of the Cold War, episodes draw on contemporary tensions, lending its stories a sense of immediacy and plausibility. The stakes feel real because they are grounded in real-world concerns. Victory rarely takes the form of a clear resolution. More often, it consists of preventing something worse from occurring.

In July 1979, while preparing the third season, Mackintosh disappeared under circumstances that remain unresolved. He was aboard a small aircraft over the Gulf of Alaska with Susan Insole and pilot Graham Barber when the plane vanished. A distress signal was received, but no wreckage or survivors were ever found. The mystery deepened when it emerged the aircraft had made an unexplained stop at an abandoned World War II airfield before continuing its journey.

Mackintosh left behind four completed scripts, including the intended conclusion of *The Sandbaggers*. Although other writers were brought in to complete the season, the distinctive voice and intricate structure defining the show proved difficult to sustain. The show was soon cancelled, bringing an abrupt end to one of the most rigorous espionage dramas ever produced. Robert G. Folsom's biography *The Life and Mysterious Death of Ian Mackintosh* later examined both his career and the circumstances surrounding his disappearance.

A small number of tie-in novels extended *The Sandbaggers* beyond television. One adapted material from the first season, while *The Sandbaggers: Think of a Number*, written under the pseudonym Donald Lancaster by William Marshall, presented an original story. The novel captures the tone and structure of the series with notable accuracy, reinforcing its emphasis on decision-making, consequence, and control.

The influence of *The Sandbaggers* extended beyond its original run. In 2001, Greg Rucka launched *Queen and Country*, a comic series built on similar foundations of political maneuvering, moral compromise, and operational consequence. Like Mackintosh's work, it centers on the Special Operations Section, with operatives known as minders navigating a world defined by pressure and uncertainty. The series expanded into graphic novels and prose works, continuing the thematic lineage established decades earlier.

Both *The Sandbaggers* and *Queen and Country* share a central key. Intelligence work is not defined by action, but by decisions. It is shaped by incomplete information, competing priorities, and the knowledge a choice made in a quiet office may place someone in immediate danger.

The Sandbaggers brings that reality into focus, revealing the burden carried by those who determine when and how intelligence is acted upon. The work is controlled, deliberate, and often invisible, yet its consequences extend far beyond the rooms in which decisions are made.

Responsibility within this world is rarely straightforward. It is shared, deferred, and sometimes avoided, yet it remains present in every choice, shaping the actions that follow and the outcomes that cannot be undone.

SPOOKS (MI5)—THE TEAM

The end of the Cold War did not bring espionage to a close. It changed its shape. By the early 2000s, threats had shifted, the pace had accelerated, and intelligence work had become more visible than at any point in its history. Technology replaced many traditional methods, while political scrutiny increased and public awareness expanded. *Spooks*, known in the United States as *MI5*, captures this transition, presenting intelligence work as immediate, interconnected, and rarely confined to a single operation or a single point of failure.

Premiering on the BBC in 2002 and running for ten seasons, the series presents intelligence work as a continuous state of urgency. It follows a group of MI5 officers based at Thames House as they respond to terrorist plots, espionage activity, cyber threats, political crises, and internal security failures. Unlike earlier espionage dramas centered on a single dominant figure, *Spooks* is built as an ensemble. The team evolves over time as characters are killed, reassigned, exposed, or forced out, reinforcing a central truth of modern intelligence work. No one is indispensable, and no one is completely safe.

At the center of the series for much of its run is Harry Pearce, head of Section D, played by Peter Firth. Harry occupies a position bridging leadership and accountability. He is not a field operative and not an executioner. His role is to manage people, allocate resources, and make decisions carrying immediate consequences. Unlike Burnside in *The Sandbaggers*, Harry does not operate within a small, tightly controlled unit. He oversees a broader, more fluid organization, one in which decisions must be made quickly and often with incomplete information.

Within British espionage drama, *Spooks* represents the team. Intelligence work is no longer defined by a single professional or even by a single controlling figure. It is distributed across a network of specialists, each responsible for a specific function. Field officers such as Tom Quinn and later Adam Carter conduct surveillance, recruit informants, and engage directly with threats. Analysts like Ruth Evershed interpret vast streams of data, identifying patterns otherwise invisible. Technical specialists manage communications, surveillance systems, and cyber operations. Administrative staff coordinate logistics and maintain the structure allowing the organization to function. The result is a model of intelligence work that depends on integration rather than individual action.

Integration introduces its own strain. Information passes through multiple hands, and each transfer creates the possibility of delay, distortion, or failure. Decisions are made under pressure, often before the full picture is clear. Trust becomes essential, not only between individuals, but across the organization itself. When trust falters, even briefly, the consequences spread quickly, affecting operations that depend on coordination at every level.

Spooks operates at speed within this system. Information moves rapidly, often in real time, and decisions must follow with equal urgency. There is little opportunity for prolonged analysis or careful deliberation. Situations develop quickly, and the margin for error is narrow. A constant sense of pressure follows, not only within individual episodes but across the series as a whole. The work is not episodic in the traditional sense. It is continuous, with each decision feeding into the next.

The series also places a strong emphasis on consequence. From its earliest episodes, it establishes that characters are vulnerable. One of the most memorable early storylines ends with a sudden and brutal death, signaling this is not a world governed by narrative protection. Agents are injured, careers collapse, and personal relationships disintegrate under the strain of secrecy and responsibility. The cost of the work is not abstract. It is immediate and personal.

A cumulative effect takes hold. The work does not reset at the end of an episode. Decisions carry forward, shaping future operations and altering relationships within the team. Trust builds and erodes over time, and constant exposure to risk begins to wear down judgment. The series suggests the greatest threat is not always external, but the gradual strain placed on those required to make decisions without pause.

The changing nature of intelligence work is reflected in the types of threats the team faces. Much of the action takes place within the United Kingdom rather than in distant foreign locations. The adversaries are not always external agents, but individuals operating within British society, motivated by ideology, grievance, or opportunity. This shift brings the work closer to home, increasing both its urgency and its complexity.

Technology plays a central role in this environment. Mobile communications, surveillance systems, financial tracking, and cyber operations are integral to many investigations. Information is gathered and processed at a scale earlier intelligence services could not have imagined. Reliance on technology introduces new vulnerabilities. Systems can be compromised, data manipulated, and the speed of information can overwhelm the ability to interpret it accurately.

Despite its modern setting, *Spooks* remains connected to traditions established by earlier British espionage dramas. The work still revolves around responsibility, compromise, and decisions affecting lives. Harry Pearce, like Burnside before him, carries the burden of those decisions. The shift appears in the complexity of the environment. He must manage not only operations, but also interactions between individuals, departments, and external pressures, all influencing the outcome of a case.

A small number of tie-in publications expanded the world beyond the series. Companion volumes such as *Spooks Confidential* and *The Personnel Files* presented the organization through dossiers, interviews, and internal records. Rather than extending individual stories, these works reinforce the idea of MI5 as a functioning system, with depth, continuity, and institutional memory.

What *Spooks* ultimately demonstrates is that modern intelligence work is not the responsibility of a single individual. It depends on coordination across roles, disciplines, and layers of authority. Analysts, field officers, technical specialists, and administrators must function as part of a unified system, each contributing to an outcome no one person could achieve alone.

The individual still matters, but the work is no longer centered on one perspective. It is distributed across teams and departments, shaped by overlapping responsibilities and shared pressures. The organization becomes visible, not as background, but as the subject itself.

Spooks presents espionage as a collective effort defined by urgency, interconnection, and constant adaptation. Information moves quickly, decisions are made under pressure, and the outcome depends on how effectively the system operates as a whole.

SMILEY—THE STRATEGIST

Intelligence work does not always take place in the field. George Smiley operates in that world. In the television adaptations of John le Carré's novels, he neither carries out operations nor issues direct orders. He understands how the game is played. His work unfolds slowly, often invisibly, shaped by patience, memory, and an ability to recognize patterns others overlook or dismiss.

Smiley first came to television in BBC adaptations of le Carré's novels, most notably *Tinker Tailor Soldier Spy* and later *Smiley's People*. Portrayed by Alec Guinness in one of the most controlled and intelligent performances on television, Smiley is not an obvious hero. He is middle-aged, soft-spoken, physically unremarkable, and frequently underestimated. He does not resemble the conventional image of a spy, and that is precisely what makes him effective.

Within British television espionage, Smiley represents the strategist. His focus is not on a single operation or a single agent. He works at the level of systems, networks, and long-term deception. Where Callan confronts a target and Burnside manages an operation, Smiley studies the entire board, considering how each move connects to those that came before and those that will follow.

The world he inhabits is the Circus, le Carré's thinly veiled version of MI6. It is a place of committees, rival departments, internal politics, and institutional memory. Beneath that structure runs a quieter conflict, one fought through informants, double agents, and carefully constructed lies. Smiley's primary tools are not weapons or force, but attention and endurance. He reads old files, revisits past operations, interviews retired agents, and listens closely to what is said and what is avoided. From these fragments, he assembles a coherent reality of events others have failed to grasp.

Smiley understands the work at a deeper level than most fictional spies. Intelligence is not about dramatic victories. It is about limiting damage, preserving advantage, and avoiding catastrophe. His principal adversary, the Soviet spymaster Karla, is not a theatrical villain but a professional counterpart, operating under similar constraints on the opposite side. Their conflict unfolds not through confrontation, but through a prolonged contest of strategy, each move calculated, each loss weighed against a larger objective.

Smiley's methods are quiet, but they are not gentle. He is prepared to sacrifice agents, careers, and reputations when necessary to protect a more valuable source or secure a broader strategic position. These decisions are not taken lightly, but they are accepted as part of the responsibility he carries. Like Burnside, he sees how the work often requires choosing the least damaging option rather than an ideal one. The separation emerges through scale. Burnside manages immediate crises. Smiley manages long-term outcomes.

The television adaptations reflect this approach with remarkable restraint. Scenes often consist of conversations in offices, interviews conducted in subdued settings, and meetings where little appears to happen on the surface. Yet the tension is constant because each exchange carries weight. Information is tested, withheld, or revealed with care. Guinness plays Smiley as a man who absorbs everything and reveals very little. When he acts, it is deliberate and final, the result of sustained observation rather than impulse.

Unlike many series in this section, Smiley's story begins in literature rather than television. Le Carré, drawing on his own experience in intelligence, created the character across a sequence of novels including *Call for the Dead*, *A Murder of Quality*, *The Spy Who Came in from the Cold*, *Tinker Tailor Soldier Spy*, *The Honourable Schoolboy*, and *Smiley's People*. These works form one of the most significant bodies of espionage fiction, and the television adaptations are notable for preserving their tone, complexity, and moral ambiguity.

What le Carré understood, and what the Smiley stories convey with clarity, is that intelligence work extends beyond individual agents or operations. It is shaped by governments, ideology, institutional pressure, and the gradual erosion of certainty. Smiley is not only confronting external adversaries. He is managing internal divisions, protecting fragile sources, and navigating an environment where loyalty is often uncertain and motives are rarely transparent.

Within the broader structure of British espionage drama, Smiley occupies the highest level of the profession. He sees the full extent of the system. Beneath him are the controllers directing sections, the operatives carrying out assignments, and the analysts interpreting information. Smiley rarely leaves London, yet his decisions influence actions across countries and continents.

George Smiley represents a longer view of intelligence, one shaped by patience and experience rather than urgency. His work develops over time, connecting details that might otherwise remain isolated and incomplete. Meaning emerges gradually, built through observation and reflection.

He recognizes the system, but also its limitations. Strategy can guide events, but it cannot fully control them. Even the most careful planning must eventually give way to action, and when it does, the outcome is never entirely certain.

THE PROFESSIONALS—THE ENFORCERS

Intelligence work reaches a point where planning and strategy give way to action. Operations fail, threats escalate, and time runs out. In those moments, governments turn to specialists trained to respond quickly and decisively. *The Professionals* occupies that space, following the agents of CI5 as they confront situations that cannot be resolved through analysis or negotiation alone.

When British television shifted into a harder, faster, more dangerous gear in the late 1970s, *The Professionals* arrived in 1977 with force—loud, stylish, and unapologetically violent in a way audiences had rarely seen before. Produced by Brian Clemens, the series follows agents of CI5, a fictional branch of British law enforcement tasked with handling terrorism, espionage, and organized crime. What set the show apart was not only the action, but the attitude. The world of CI5 is cynical, dangerous, and constantly in motion, and the men who operate within it match that intensity.

At the center of the series are three distinct figures. Gordon Jackson portrays George Cowley, the disciplined and pragmatic head of CI5, a former intelligence officer who runs the unit with authority and a dry, measured wit. Martin Shaw plays Ray Doyle, intense, physical, and often driven by instinct, bringing a police background and emotional edge to the work. Lewis Collins plays William Bodie, a former soldier and mercenary, controlled, confident, and willing to bend rules when necessary. Together, they form a combination of command, volatility, and force, one of the most recognizable trios in action television.

Within British espionage drama, CI5 represents enforcement. These are not individuals who gather intelligence or debate policy. They are deployed when a situation has become too urgent or too dangerous for quiet solutions. They deal directly with terrorists, armed criminals, foreign operatives, and internal threats requiring immediate response. Where Smiley studies the board and Burnside directs the pieces, Bodie and Doyle are sent in when the situation is already in motion and control is slipping.

The Professionals runs on momentum. Episodes move quickly, dialogue is sharp, and the action sequences carry an energy more commonly associated with cinema than television of the time. Car chases became a defining element, particularly the recurring image of Bodie's gold Ford Capri sliding through corners and crashing through barriers in pursuit of suspects. These sequences are not incidental. They define the visual identity of the series and establish a new standard for televised action.

The show expands the boundaries of violence and realism. Criminals are not always captured cleanly. Confrontations are sudden, often chaotic, and sometimes unresolved. Storylines involve political extremism, international crime networks, espionage activity, and corruption within institutions. The result is a harder, more immediate tone than many of its contemporaries. Danger is not abstract. It is physical, immediate, and often unavoidable.

A series of tie-in novels extended the show's reach during its original run. Published under the house name Ken Blake, these books adapted episodes rather than presenting new stories, preserving the tone and pace of the series in prose form and keeping the characters active between broadcasts.

The chemistry between Shaw and Collins contributes significantly to the show's success. Doyle and Bodie argue, challenge each other, and compete, but they also rely on one another when operations turn dangerous. Their partnership combines tension and familiarity, creating a dynamic that would influence later action series and films. Cowley, positioned above them, provides a stabilizing presence, both in the operational realities and the political pressures shaping their assignments. The influence of *The Professionals* is easy to trace in later television. The model of two contrasting operatives working within a semi-autonomous government unit reappears in numerous forms. Fast vehicles, tightly constructed dialogue, and morally complex assignments become standard features of action programming in the decades that follow. Later productions may have larger budgets or more elaborate effects, but the essential structure is already established here.

Decades later, the concept returned in *The New Professionals*, a reboot that reimagined CI5 within a more contemporary framework. Starring Edward Woodward as Harry Malone, the son of a colleague of Cowley, the series introduced a new generation of operatives facing international terrorism and organized crime. The presence of Woodward, closely associated with *Callan*, creates a connection between earlier and later phases of British espionage television. Although the revival did not achieve the same cultural impact as the original, it demonstrates the durability of the concept.

More than four decades after its debut, *The Professionals* remains one of the most influential British action series. Its combination of character dynamics, rapid pacing, and physical confrontation reshaped expectations of what television action could deliver. Within the broader structure of espionage drama, its role is precise. *The Professionals* occupies the point at which planning gives way to execution. When time has run out and control is no longer sufficient, the response becomes immediate and visible. The work is no longer concealed. It unfolds in motion, under pressure, and often in full view. It represents a distinct function within the same system, one operating alongside analysis and strategy, but under entirely different conditions.

MAN IN A SUITCASE—THE OUTSIDER

Intelligence officers can be removed from the system, discarded, or pushed outside it without warning. The skills remain. The structure does not. *Man in a Suitcase* follows John McGill, a man forced to navigate a world where he no longer belongs to any service, yet still carries the instincts he believes defined him.

While top-tier British espionage series such as *Callan* and *The Sandbaggers* receive much of the attention from students of serious spy television, there is a third series that belongs in the same conversation, even if discussed less often. *Man in a Suitcase* takes the espionage hero and reshapes him into something more complicated, a man without a country, without a service, and without a safety net.

For thirty episodes broadcast between September 1967 and April 1968, Richard Bradford played John McGill, an American intelligence agent falsely accused of treason and discarded by his own people. The accusation destroys both his career and his reputation, leaving him stranded in London and working as a freelance investigator and occasional intelligence operative for anyone able to meet his fee of five hundred dollars a day plus expenses. He travels constantly, carrying everything he owns in a single suitcase, moving from job to job and country to country, never remaining anywhere long enough to belong.

Within British television espionage, McGill represents the outsider. He is no longer part of the system, yet he cannot escape it. He still operates in the same world of informants, agents, criminals, and intelligence officers, but without protection, backup, or official recognition. He is what remains when the system decides a man is expendable and the man survives.

That premise distinguishes the series. Most television spies work for governments and answer to superiors. McGill works for himself. Most television detectives have an office, a partner, or a badge. McGill has none of these. He exists in a state of permanent displacement, and the series uses that condition as its foundation. He is not simply completing assignments. He is navigating a life defined by exclusion.

Part of the tension running through the series comes from the reason McGill cannot clear his name. Any serious attempt to expose the truth would result in the exposure, torture, and likely execution of a double agent still operating inside the Soviet Union. His freedom and reputation are tied directly to another man's survival, forcing him to remain the scapegoat for a crime he did not commit. That constraint gives the series a moral dimension extending beyond the immediate plot of any individual episode.

Richard Bradford was an unusual choice for the lead, and that quality defines the performance. A method actor with a rough edge and a tendency toward a Brando-like delivery, Bradford presents McGill as a chain-smoking, hard-drinking professional who expects to be beaten up at least once per episode and prepares accordingly. He mumbles, he shrugs, absorbs punishment, and continues. He is not polished like John Drake in *Danger Man*. He is not bureaucratic like the men in *The Sandbaggers*. He is not controlled like Callan. McGill is a brawler and a survivor, an antihero with a personal code and very little patience for authority.

What makes *Man in a Suitcase* particularly distinctive is the way it blends private eye fiction with espionage. In many episodes, McGill operates as a classic American private detective, taking cases, locating missing individuals, and dealing with criminals at street level. In others, he is drawn back into intelligence work, confronting former colleagues, enemy agents, and the political realities that shaped his downfall. The result is a hybrid series, combining elements of spy fiction and hardboiled detective narrative.

A single tie-in novel extended the series beyond television. *The Sleeping Cupid*, written under the name E. G. Whitney, presents an original story rather than adapting an episode, capturing McGill's voice and perspective with notable accuracy.

Unlike many British series of the 1960s, *Man in a Suitcase* survives in excellent condition and has been released on DVD in both the United Kingdom and the United States. Viewed today, it holds up remarkably well, largely because the central character does not depend on gadgets or spectacle. The series works because McGill works, grounded in performance and premise rather than production scale.

Within the larger landscape of British television espionage, *Man in a Suitcase* occupies a unique position. It is neither fully a spy series nor entirely a private detective series, but something between the two. More significantly, it is one of the earliest television explorations of the disavowed agent, the operative cut loose by his own side and forced to continue alone. That concept would later become familiar in film and television, but in 1967 it was still developing.

John McGill moves through Europe with one suitcase, a gun, and a damaged reputation. He works for those who will hire him, trusts very few people, and keeps moving because stopping would mean confronting what has been taken from him. He is no longer part of the system, but he cannot fully escape its influence.

McGill exists outside the structure that once defined him. The system is gone, but the habits remain. He works alone, applying the same skills without the support or authority that once accompanied them. It is a more uncertain existence, shaped by independence rather than assignment, and by necessity rather than direction.

SLOW HORSES—THE DISCARDED

Every intelligence organization creates its margins. Not everyone is dismissed, and not everyone is trusted. Some are kept at a distance, assigned work barely sufficient to justify their presence. In *Slow Horses*, Slough House serves as a holding ground for agents who have made mistakes, caused problems, or become inconvenient. They remain part of the system, but only barely. The focus falls on those still inside it, positioned at the outer edge, neither trusted nor entirely removed.

Premiering in 2022 and based on the novels of Mick Herron, *Slow Horses* brings British espionage television into the modern era while remaining connected to traditions established by earlier series such as *Callan*, *The Sandbaggers*, and the Smiley adaptations. The series follows a group of disgraced or sidelined MI5 officers assigned to Slough House, a dumping ground for failed agents and bureaucratic embarrassments, overseen by the foul-mouthed, disheveled, and deceptively capable Jackson Lamb.

Within British television espionage, the slow horses represent the discarded. They are not active field agents, not trusted controllers, and not respected analysts. They are the people the system has decided are no longer useful, or at least not useful enough to be trusted with meaningful work. Their days are spent pushing paper, reviewing minor reports, and completing administrative tasks designed less to produce results than to encourage resignation. Slough House is not a formal punishment. It is a quiet mechanism for ending careers without acknowledgment.

What makes *Slow Horses* effective is that those sent to Slough House are not incompetent. Many are capable officers who made a single mistake at the wrong moment. River Cartwright, for example, begins the series by mishandling a training exercise and is quickly reassigned despite clear ability. Others carry different liabilities—alcohol problems, anger issues, or a history of insubordination. Some were simply on the wrong side of an internal political struggle. What they share is a loss of trust. The system has not eliminated them, but set them aside. The arrangement reveals how intelligence organizations function. Failure is not treated as an anomaly. It is managed. Slough House exists to contain mistakes, isolate them from the operational center while still extracting whatever value remains. The individuals assigned there serve as reminders of what follows when judgment falters or priorities shift. Their presence allows the larger organization to maintain the appearance of control, even as it absorbs the consequences of its own decisions.

At the center of this environment is Jackson Lamb, played with deliberate weariness and sharp-edged authority by Gary Oldman. Lamb presents himself as indifferent, abrasive, and frequently offensive, yet beneath that exterior remains a highly skilled intelligence officer with a clear grasp of how the system operates. He protects his team in his own manner, not out of sentiment, but because he recognizes the purpose Slough House serves. It exists to absorb mistakes and shield those higher in the hierarchy from consequence. Lamb represents what long exposure to the system produces—a man who has seen enough to discard any illusion of institutional nobility while continuing to function within it.

Unlike earlier espionage series focusing on individuals at the height of their effectiveness, *Slow Horses* concentrates on what follows failure. It examines stalled careers, damaged reputations, and individuals forced to continue working within a structure that no longer values them. The work assigned to Slough House appears insignificant, yet often develops into something more substantial. Minor cases reveal larger problems, and the people considered least reliable are frequently the ones who uncover what others have missed.

The impact builds over time. Assignment to Slough House is not simply a professional setback. It alters how individuals see themselves and how others see them. Confidence erodes, initiative is discouraged, and expectations are lowered. Over time, the environment can diminish judgment as effectively as any external pressure. Yet it can also produce a different kind of resilience. Those who remain learn to operate without recognition, support, or the expectation success will be acknowledged. When opportunity arises, they act not because they are expected to, but because the work still demands it.

The series draws from Herron's novels, beginning with *Slow Horses* and continuing through *Dead Lions*, *Real Tigers*, *Spook Street*, *London Rules*, *Joe Country*, *Slough House*, and *Bad Actors*, among others. Across these books, Herron constructs a detailed portrayal of modern intelligence work shaped by internal politics, bureaucratic maneuvering, damaged careers, and intermittent bursts of genuine danger. The television adaptation captures this tone effectively, balancing dark humor, abrupt violence, and persistent skepticism about how intelligence organizations function in practice.

Slow Horses contributes to the broader tradition of British espionage television by acknowledging that the system produces not only professionals, controllers, and strategists, but also failures. Not every career concludes with advancement or recognition. Some end in offices removed from influence, with limited responsibility and little expectation. Yet those individuals retain the skills that once defined them, and under the right circumstances, those skills become relevant again.

Slough House occupies the far edge of the intelligence world, a place for those who remain in the system but no longer fully belong to it. Careers have faltered, trust has diminished, and expectations have been lowered. The system does not entirely discard them. It keeps them in reserve, a reminder that even within a profession built on control, margins remain where things do not fit, and where the overlooked can still matter.

CASE SUMMARY

Unlike the working detective, who operates in the open, the intelligence operative works in ambiguity. This distinction may be the most important dividing line between the two professions. The detective seeks to prove something. The intelligence officer seeks to learn something. One works toward evidence, the other toward information. One builds a case, the other assembles a picture.

British television has long understood espionage is not about gadgets or gunfights, despite what more spectacular stories suggest. At its core, intelligence work depends on patience, judgment, and an intimate knowledge of people. Information rarely arrives in a clear or complete form. It emerges through conversations, overheard remarks, stolen documents, recruited agents, and careful observation. The intelligence officer must constantly evaluate what is true, what is false, and what is intended to mislead. In this respect, the intelligence officer and the detective are not far apart. Both seek to understand what actually happened, but they do so under very different conditions.

The intelligence world is also one in which success is often invisible. When a detective solves a murder, the result is public. When an intelligence officer prevents an event, there may be no record of what was avoided. Espionage becomes a peculiar profession, defined as much by absence as by action. It is a world of secrecy, but also one of reports, briefings, committees, and long stretches of waiting. British television consistently emphasizes this quieter reality, showing meetings and analysis matter as much as fieldwork.

Loyalty in these stories is rarely straightforward. It exists in layers, loyalty to country, to colleagues, to sources, and at times to individuals who may themselves be compromised. Intelligence work requires decisions made with incomplete information, and those decisions often carry consequences that cannot be undone. A detective may make an arrest and see the outcome tested in court. An intelligence officer may act on uncertainty and never know the full result.

These series present espionage as a profession defined less by action than by responsibility. The responsibility to judge information, to decide who can be trusted, and to determine when to act and when to wait. Perhaps most difficult is the responsibility of knowing things that cannot be shared.

By the end of these stories, the intelligence officer appears less as a figure of glamour and more as a professional observer, someone who watches, listens, and attempts to anticipate events before they unfold. In this respect, the distance between the spy and the detective begins to narrow. Both work with information, depend on informants, conduct interviews, whether called interrogations or debriefings, write reports, and attempt to understand motive, opportunity, and human weakness. The contrast is in purpose. One is trying to prevent threats to the state. The other is trying to resolve crimes against the public.

Understanding investigation as a profession requires both worlds. The world of secrets and the world of arrests. The world of information and the world of evidence. The intelligence officer works in shadow, while the detective works in the open, and it is there, in the open, that the next part of this book begins.

PART TWO

THE WORKING DETECTIVES

Investigating the police—the men and women who work cases, make arrests, write reports, and testify in court.

INTRODUCTION—FROM FIRST CALL TO LAST CASE

While the espionage officer operates in the shadows, the working detective operates in full view, under fluorescent lights, in rain, in traffic, in interview rooms, and in the long gray hours between one cup of tea and the next. British television has always understood the distinction. The spy may carry the burden of national security, but the working detective carries something more immediate and more constant, the daily responsibility of order, paperwork, victims, supervisors, and the slow machinery of the law.

The difference is not only visibility, but accountability. The intelligence officer may act without recognition. The detective works in a system where every action must be explained, recorded, and justified. Decisions are reviewed. Evidence is tested. Cases succeed or fail in public. The work is shaped as much by procedure as by instinct, and by the requirement conclusions hold under scrutiny.

This section is not about individual programs. It is about a profession. British television, more consistently than any other, has treated policing as a layered occupation with its own hierarchy, internal divisions, and pressures. Rank matters. Uniform matters. CID matters. Who answers the call, who knocks on the door, who conducts the interview, who signs the report, who receives the promotion, and who absorbs the consequences all matter. The series gathered here are not grouped by popularity or memory, but by function. Each represents a role within the larger structure of British policing, and, in one case, what happens when the career ends but the detective does not.

The uniform officer is the visible face of the law, arriving first and often with the least information. The initial response is uncertain, shaped by what is encountered on arrival. From there, the work divides. The provincial CID officer deals with cases drawn from community, history, and relationships built over years or generations. The Flying Squad operates at speed, responding to robbery and violence where hesitation carries risk. These are not simply different assignments. They are different approaches, shaped by the demands of the task.

Partnership adds another layer. Two detectives may stand in the same place and reach different conclusions, each bringing a distinct perspective to the problem. The difference can create friction, but it can also produce clarity. In more complex cases, the structure expands further. The murder squad marks the point at which investigation becomes coordinated effort, where multiple lines of inquiry must be managed at once, and where pressure does not ease with time.

Some roles are defined by tension within the system itself. Internal Affairs investigates its own, operating in an environment where cooperation is limited and trust is uncertain. The work requires distance, judgment, and a willingness to question the institution from within. Other figures reflect the accumulation of experience. The seasoned detective carries years of work in memory and approach, relying less on speed and more on recognition. The wartime detective operates under conditions where the law coexists with national necessity, altering priorities and complicating decisions.

As the structure evolves, so does the work. The modern detective faces an environment shaped by oversight, media attention, legal challenge, and increasing complexity. The job is no longer confined to station or street. It extends into systems that monitor, record, and evaluate every stage of an investigation. In that environment, the detective manages not only the case, but the conditions under which it is conducted.

What remains when the career ends? Retirement does not erase experience. Cases linger. Decisions remain. The detective who steps away does not necessarily leave the work behind. In some instances, it resumes, not as obligation, but as unfinished business.

Across these variations, one principle remains constant. There is no single kind of detective, only different assignments, pressures, personalities, and points within a career. A constable on patrol in the early 1960s worked in a world defined by local knowledge and limited resources. A senior investigator in the 1980s operated within a more formal structure. A modern detective works in an environment shaped by policy, oversight, and public visibility. Each would recognize the job, but not entirely the conditions in which it is done.

British television reflects these changes with consistency. Authority shifts. Methods develop. The relationship between police and public evolves. The way detectives speak, both to suspects and to each other, adapts over time. What remains is the requirement to manage uncertainty and move a case forward despite incomplete information.

Most police work is not defined by action. It is defined by persistence. Knocking on the same door more than once. Waiting for results that may or may not clarify the situation. Writing reports, reviewing statements, managing informants, dealing with supervisors. Accepting that some cases do not resolve cleanly and some answers remain partial. The strongest of these series understand that the work is built on repetition and attention, not spectacle.

Place shapes the profession. London presents different challenges from Glasgow. Glasgow differs from a rural county. A wartime coastal town operates under different pressures than a modern city under scrutiny. Crime shifts with environment, and the detective adjusts with it. A provincial officer may rely on familiarity. A specialist unit depends on speed and coordination. An Internal Affairs investigator operates in isolation. Each role reflects its surroundings.

Taken together, the series in this section form an informal map of the British police profession as presented through television drama. Not exact, not official, but often close enough to suggest how the system functions in practice. Rank carries both privilege and responsibility. CID is respected and resented. Specialists and uniform officers view the job from different angles. Supervisors consider budgets and consequences. Detectives focus on cases. At the center are victims, witnesses, and suspects, each bringing a version of events.

The working detective operates in that space. Not in the shadows, and not in the spotlight. The work takes place between the crime and the report, between what is known and what can be proven. British television has spent decades examining that ground, creating a body of work that approaches a professional study presented in the form of drama.

Z-CARS—THE UNIFORMS

When *Z-Cars* arrived on British television in 1962, it did more than introduce a new police series. It altered how the police officer was seen. The familiar figure of the local bobby—the steady presence who knew every face on his beat—gave way to something less predictable. These officers worked unfamiliar streets, dealt with people they did not know, and faced situations that did not settle with a quiet word. Crime felt immediate, uncertain, and at times dangerous. British television began to present policing as work rather than reassurance.

Set in a fictional area near Liverpool and based loosely on conditions in Lancashire, the series presented a world where policing was neither picturesque nor comfortable. Officers drove fast, argued among themselves, dealt with uncooperative suspects, and spent much of their time on domestic disputes, drunk and disorderly calls, petty thefts, and sudden violence. The setting was noisy, crowded, and unpredictable. This was not the countryside. This was modern Britain, and it required a different kind of policing.

One of the most important shifts was structural. Policing became a team effort rather than a lone figure on a bicycle. Patrol cars, radio communication, and coordinated response moved to the center. Officers no longer relied on familiarity with a beat. They responded to calls, crossed wider areas, and dealt with situations they had not anticipated minutes earlier. The work became reactive as well as preventive, and mobility carried equal weight with knowledge.

The series also introduced a defining element of later British police drama. It presented officers as human. They made mistakes, lost tempers, disagreed with supervisors, and went home tired before returning to do it again. Paperwork, discipline, and rank shaped the job as much as the street. The station was not a backdrop. It was a workplace, with routines, tensions, and expectations. That emphasis on procedure and hierarchy established a template later series would refine.

The portrayal of the public shifted as well. Earlier programs often presented citizens as cooperative and respectful. Here, they could be angry, frightened, dishonest, or simply unhelpful. The police no longer operated within a polite, orderly society. They worked in a country shaped by youth culture, economic pressure, class tension, and rising urban crime. The series does not argue the police were always right, but it makes clear the work was necessary and often thankless.

The visual style reinforced the approach. Shot in a semi-documentary manner, often on location and with a looser camera, *Z-Cars* feels direct and sometimes chaotic. Scenes overlap. Conversations unfold without polish. Events do not always resolve neatly. Officers arrive late, detain the wrong person, or return and begin again. This marked a break from the tidy, self-contained storytelling of earlier police dramas.

The realism was not imagined. One of the key technical advisers, William Prendergast, served as a Detective Sergeant with Liverpool City Police. Joining the force in 1928, he spent thirty-one years in service and received twenty-two commendations. He worked some of the toughest urban divisions and later served in Special Branch, where his duties brought him into contact with

Liverpool's Chinese community. After retirement, he moved onto the series as adviser, contributing plots drawn from experience and working on set and location to maintain authenticity. He bridged older forms of policing and the modern practices the series depicted.

The connection between television and print followed. Three tie-in paperbacks appeared—*Z Cars* by Troy Kennedy Martin (1962), *Z Cars Again* by Allan Prior (1963), and *Z Cars—Barlow on Trial* by Ian Kennedy Martin (1965). These were adaptations of early scripts, preserving representative stories in prose and reinforcing the link between television drama and written narrative.

Prendergast extended that link further with three books drawn from his own cases: *Z-Car Detective*, *Calling All Z-Cars*, and *Z-Car Squad*. These works complement the series and its adaptations, forming a small body of material grounded in actual police work. The series was not simply inspired by policing. It was built from it.

Equally important, *Z-Cars* demonstrated how little of police work is glamorous. Much of the job consists of routine calls, minor offenses, and paperwork. But routine can turn without warning. A domestic dispute escalates. A traffic stop becomes a pursuit. A missing person leads somewhere more serious. That unpredictability became a defining feature of later British police drama.

Z-Cars forms the foundation of modern British police television. Without it, there is likely no *Softly, Softly*, no *The Sweeney*, no *Juliet Bravo*, no *A Touch of Frost*. It established that police drama could focus on procedure, personality, and pressure rather than resolution before the final break. It also confirmed the station as central, because it is where decisions are made, reports written, and careers shaped.

The series marks the point where the myth of the *Dixon of Dock Green* bobby gives way to the modern police officer. The job grows more complex. Cities expand. Society shifts. The police become more mobile, more organized, more professional, and more bureaucratic, with increasing distance from the older idea of the local constable who knew everyone by name.

The officers in *Z-Cars* are not symbols. They are working police officers. They answer calls, make arrests, file reports, and respond to whatever comes over the radio next. The series belongs at the beginning of this section because it shows the job at the point of contact, where public and police meet.

From there, the work moves inward. The patrol car leaves. Statements are taken. Evidence is logged. Cases begin to take shape. What starts on the street continues in quieter spaces, where progress depends on patience, structure, and the ability to turn an incident into a case.

SOFTLY, SOFTLY—PROVINCIAL CID

Policing does not end with an arrest. Once a suspect is in custody, the work often begins. *Softly, Softly* and its successor *Softly, Softly: Task Force* shift attention from street to station, from action to process. Investigations are constructed step by step through interviews, reports, and coordination. The series opens the structure behind policing, meetings, case conferences, and layers of supervision turning incidents into organized inquiries.

Where *Z-Cars* is built on response, *Softly, Softly* is grounded in investigation. The patrol car gives way to the office, the interview room, and the incident board. The series follows senior officers, most notably Barlow and Watt, as they supervise inquiries, coordinate detectives, and manage the administrative and political realities surrounding major cases. This is a different form of police drama. Tension comes not from sirens or pursuit, but from assembling a case, directing personnel, and making decisions able to withstand scrutiny in court and from superiors.

More clearly than many predecessors, the series presents policing as a structured system. Not a collection of individual detectives solving isolated crimes, but a chain of command, a network of departments, and a process where each stage depends on the one before it. The detective is no longer a lone figure following instinct. He is part of a team, and that team answers to a hierarchy. Authority moves downward. Responsibility moves upward.

Procedure becomes central. Interviews must be conducted correctly. Evidence logged, preserved, and presented in proper form. Statements taken with care. Warrants obtained within the law. Cases fail not because the suspect is wrong, but because the process is mishandled. The series recognizes where many real investigations succeed or collapse. It presents police work as slow, methodical, and dependent on patience rather than impulse.

As the series evolves into *Softly, Softly: Task Force*, the scope expands and emphasis shifts toward major investigations and coordinated operations. The term "task force" is revealing. It does not describe a single detective or even a single unit, but a temporary organization assembled to address a specific problem, often drawing personnel from different departments and specialties. The development adds another layer of realism, one that would become central to later police dramas. Major crime is not solved by one individual with a notebook. It is resolved through teams, shared information, coordination, and sustained effort.

The series also examines how the job changes with rank. As officers move higher in the organization, responsibilities shift. Time spent pursuing suspects gives way to managing people, resources, and expectations. Senior officers consider budgets, manpower, and whether a case justifies the resources it demands. They also weigh how outcomes will be viewed by superiors and the public. The work becomes less visible, but no less demanding.

Like several British police series of the period, *Softly, Softly* moved from television to print. Two paperback tie-ins were published by Pan Books: *Softly Softly* (1966) by Paula Byrne and *Softly Softly Casebook* (1967) by Allan Prior. Both adapt material from the series rather than presenting original narratives. Their existence reflects how strongly the program was identified with procedural storytelling. The title *Casebook* is particularly fitting, as the series often feels less like conventional drama and more like a dramatized account of how investigations unfold.

Within the broader history of British television, *Softly, Softly* and *Task Force* mark a shift. Police drama moves away from the individual problem solver and toward policing as an organized system. This is the world of briefing rooms, wall maps, typed reports, and case conferences. One officer interviews a witness, another checks alibis, another coordinates with uniform units, while a senior officer ensures the investigation continues without losing procedural integrity.

Z-Cars shows what the police do. *Softly, Softly* shows how the work is done. Behind every arrest lies a structure. Behind that structure, procedure, supervision, and documentation. The series may lack the outward urgency of pursuit and confrontation, but it comes closer to how major investigations succeed.

Within this section, *Softly, Softly / Task Force* represents the rise of procedure, structure, and bureaucracy, the point where British television recognizes solving crime is not simply about identifying a suspect, but about building a case able to withstand the system in which it will be tested.

Investigations here move with care. They build through accumulation, through detail, through decisions made in sequence. Yet policing does not always allow that pace. Some crimes demand speed. Some suspects resist. Some encounters turn without warning. When that happens, the work shifts again, away from measured construction and toward something faster, more direct, and less forgiving.

THE SWEENEY—THE FLYING SQUAD

Speed defines certain kinds of policing. Armed robbery, organized crews, and mobile criminals leave little room for delay. By the mid-1970s, British television was ready to present that reality, a form of policing built on urgency, confrontation, and rapid response. *The Sweeney* brought that world to the screen, following the Flying Squad as they pursued suspects just as likely to fight back as they were to run.

When *The Sweeney* arrived in 1975, it did not ease into place. It forced its way in and pulled British crime drama into a new era of speed, grit, and attitude. Earlier police series had been measured, procedural, and often confined to the studio. This one changed the rhythm. Streets felt active, criminals dangerous, and the police recognizably human in ways television had rarely allowed. Much of the production moved onto real locations, giving the show a raw, immediate edge. Car chases tore through London streets with little polish. Fights looked sudden and painful, not staged displays but collisions. The city stopped being a backdrop and became contested ground, crowded, unstable, and always in motion.

The shift was deliberate. The production pushed away from controlled environments toward something closer to lived experience. Handheld camerawork, available light, and a pace matching the crimes being depicted created forward momentum.

Dialogue overlaps. Scenes start late and end early. Explanation gives way to movement. The result feels immediate, sometimes confrontational.

At the center stands Detective Inspector Jack Regan, played by John Thaw, with Detective Sergeant George Carter, played by Dennis Waterman. Their partnership defines the series. Regan is rough, impatient, relentless. Carter is quicker, lighter in tone, but no less committed. Together they represent the Flying Squad, the Metropolitan Police unit tasked with armed robbery and violent crime across London. Where *Softly, Softly* constructs cases, the Flying Squad interrupts them.

Tone carries as much weight as action. Regan is not a polished television detective. He drinks heavily, bends rules, pressures informants, and drives cases forward by force of will. Yet he is not presented as corrupt. He believes in results, in removing violent offenders from the street, and accepts the personal cost. The tension becomes central to later British crime drama, reflecting a view of the work as rarely clean and those doing it rarely uncomplicated.

Fatigue runs beneath the surface. Long hours, constant pressure, and the demand for results leave visible marks. Regan eats on the move, works late, and argues with superiors who expect outcomes without always acknowledging the cost. The job is not romanticized. It is relentless, and often thankless. The strain grounds the action, giving weight to every pursuit and confrontation.

The influence of *The Sweeney* is substantial. It established the template for the modern action-oriented police series, fast pacing, location shooting, sharp dialogue, and flawed central figures. Later British productions such as *The Professionals* and *Minder* followed its lead, while American television adopted elements of its style, shifting toward street-level realism and character-driven action.

Much of the impact comes from the chemistry between Thaw and Waterman. Their exchanges feel unforced, their disagreements credible, and their loyalty earned. The partnership suggests shared history, long surveillance hours, poor meals, and repeated exposure to danger. That sense of familiarity became a model for later two-hander crime narratives.

Like many successful series of the period, *The Sweeney* expanded into print. Between 1975 and 1978, Futura Publications released nine original tie-in novels. These were not retellings, but new stories extending the tone and characters into broader narratives of London's criminal world. Three were written by series creator Ian Kennedy Martin, with the remaining six by Joe Balham. A tenth book, a novelization of *The Blag*, the second feature film, was also written by Balham.

These novels form part of the series' legacy. They demonstrate the strength of its world beyond the screen. In prose, Regan and Carter operate with more room to breathe, their voices preserved through slang, dry humor, and the constant tension between procedure and the need to produce results.

Within the structure of British police television, *The Sweeney* represents the specialist unit, deployed when routine policing cannot respond quickly enough and extended investigation cannot act soon enough. The Flying Squad works between uniform patrol and CID procedure. They rely on information from detectives, support from uniform, and authorization from above, but once engaged they move fast and with considerable autonomy. This is policing at the sharp end, where mistakes carry immediate consequences and hesitation allows a suspect to disappear.

The Flying Squad marks a shift in emphasis. Work moves from response and construction to intervention. The officer is no longer waiting or building, but acting, entering the scene at speed and forcing it to resolution.

Even at full speed, action does not stand alone. Decisions still come from somewhere. Someone authorizes the move, allocates resources, defines limits. The operation may unfold on the street, but control remains elsewhere.

JULIET BRAVO—COMMAND

Authority in policing extends beyond rank. It depends on how authority is perceived, tested, and, at times, resisted. When *Juliet Bravo* arrived on British television in 1980, it introduced something rarely seen in police drama, a uniformed woman in command of a police station. The idea was not new in practice, but on television it carried weight. It required both audience and characters to reconsider what authority looked like and how it functioned.

Set in the fictional town of Hartley in Lancashire, the series follows Inspector Jean Darblay, played by Stephanie Turner, as she takes command of a rural division. From the outset, her position is not fully accepted. She is an outsider, not only to the town, but to the expectations of those she supervises. Resistance is rarely overt, yet constant, expressed through small challenges, quiet doubts, and the need to prove competence in ways her male counterparts are not required to do.

Within British television policing, Darblay represents authority at the local level, but authority that must be established rather than assumed. She is responsible for discipline, decision-making, and the overall functioning of the station, yet she must also earn the confidence of her officers and the respect of the community. The job requires more than enforcing rules. It requires interpreting them in ways that maintain both order and cooperation.

The series builds its drama through the daily realities of policing in a smaller community. Incidents emerge from local disputes, family conflicts, minor crime, and the occasional serious offense. Darblay must navigate these situations with an awareness of how closely connected the people involved are. Unlike urban policing, where anonymity can exist, this is a world in which everyone knows, or believes they know, everyone else. Decisions carry consequences beyond the immediate case, shaping relationships and reputations across the town.

Darblay's leadership centers on control, consistency, and presence. She does not rely on force or intimidation. Instead, she works through patience, observation, and a careful reading of people. She listens, assesses, and acts, often choosing solutions that preserve stability rather than simply assert authority. This does not lessen decisiveness. It sharpens it. She instinctively appreciates how policing in a community depends as much on cooperation as enforcement.

The series reflects the evolving role of women in British policing during the late twentieth century. Darblay's presence is not treated as novelty, yet it is never ignored. Her gender shapes how others respond to her, and at times how she must respond in return. She is expected to lead, but also to justify leadership in ways male officers are not. The tension between expectation and performance runs quietly through the series, adding another layer to its portrayal of authority.

Later, the role of station inspector passes to Kate Longton, played by Anna Carteret, bringing a different tone while maintaining the central idea of female leadership within a traditionally male structure. The transition reinforces that the role has become established. The question is no longer whether a woman can lead, but how that leadership is exercised.

Like several British police dramas of the period, *Juliet Bravo* extended into print, though in a more limited form. Novelizations and tie-in material were less extensive than those associated with some contemporaries, reflecting both the nature of the series and its emphasis on character and situation over action-driven plots. Its legacy rests less on expansion into other media and more on its portrayal of leadership within community policing.

Within the broader landscape of British television, *Juliet Bravo* occupies a distinct position. It focuses on authority not as a given, but as something constructed through daily interaction, consistency, and judgment. The station inspector is not removed from the work. She is part of it, responsible not only for outcomes, but for how those outcomes are achieved.

Here, policing turns on leadership. Not speed, not structure, but the ability to hold a position others may question and still make it function. Authority must be exercised, reinforced, and, at times, defended without force. The inspector stands at the center of that balance, managing officers, responding to the community, and maintaining standards. It is a role defined less by rank than by the ability to lead under constant observation.

DEMPSEY & MAKEPEACE—THE PARTNERS

Two detectives, one car, one case, and often two different ways of seeing it. Partnership sits at the center of police work, shaping how investigations move and how decisions are made. Strength comes from contrast as much as agreement, and success often depends on how those differences are handled. *Dempsey & Makepeace* builds its identity around that dynamic, pairing two officers whose methods and backgrounds rarely align, yet must function together.

Lieutenant James Dempsey, played by Michael Brandon, arrives in London from the United States and is assigned to work with Detective Sergeant Harriet Makepeace, played by Glynis Barber. The pairing creates immediate tension. Dempsey is loud, impulsive, street-focused, and impatient with procedure. Makepeace is controlled, precise, and fully aware of how the system operates. He forces entry. She secures authority. He pressures informants. She constructs the case. Each works effectively alone. Together, they become more capable than either could be individually.

The series rejects similarity as the basis for partnership. It depends on balance. One detective notices what the other overlooks. One advances, the other restrains. One engages, the other evaluates. In practice, partnerships succeed because differences serve a purpose. *Dempsey & Makepeace* turns that professional reality into both drama and, at times, humor. Beneath the style, it offers a credible view of how trust develops between investigators who begin with little reason to rely on each other.

The series reflects the direction of British police television in the mid-1980s. Pacing accelerates. Action becomes more visible. Production gains a sharper, more polished look. Chases, confrontations, and international elements appear more frequently. The style works because it is anchored in the central relationship. Viewers return as much for the interaction between Dempsey and Makepeace as for the cases themselves, watching disagreement evolve into cooperation and, eventually, professional respect.

An additional layer comes from the chemistry between Brandon and Barber, which extended beyond the series into real life. Their eventual marriage gives retrospective weight to performances already grounded in credibility. The partnership on screen feels lived-in because it is supported by something genuine, reinforcing the idea that effective working relationships depend on elements not easily reduced to method, timing, trust, and personality.

Like many successful British police series of the period, *Dempsey & Makepeace* extended into print. Six paperback tie-ins were published by Futura Books in the mid-1980s. These included *Make Peace, Not War* by Jesse Carr-Martindale, along with *Lucky Streak*, *Blind Eye*, *Jericho Scam*, and *The Bogeyman* by John Raymond, and *Love You To Death* by Jack Savage. As with similar adaptations, the novels preserved the dialogue-driven energy of the series and allowed more time with the central partnership.

Within the structure of British police drama, *Dempsey & Makepeace* represents the partnership as a working unit. It is one of the most durable frameworks in both fiction and practice. The work is dangerous, unpredictable, and often isolating. A partner serves as witness, safeguard, and sounding board, often the only person who fully understands the demands of the job. British television returns to this structure not only because it creates natural drama, but because it reflects how policing operates. Detectives rarely work alone.

Partnership introduces both friction and balance, and many investigations can be managed at that level, two officers working in concert. Some cases, however, extend beyond what two people can contain. They expand in scope, in complexity, and in consequence, requiring larger teams, coordinated effort, and a structure built to handle sustained pressure.

TAGGART—THE MURDER SQUAD

Murder changes the scale of policing. It draws more officers, more resources, and greater scrutiny from superiors and the public. What begins as a single crime becomes the responsibility of an entire team. Few British series capture that expansion more clearly than *Taggart*, where the murder squad operates under constant pressure and the reality of every decision carrying its own weight.

Set in Glasgow, *Taggart* brought a harder, bleaker tone to British crime drama. The city is not presented as postcard Scotland, but as a working environment with rough edges, industrial shadows, and crimes rooted in money, jealousy, family, and desperation. Detective Chief Inspector Jim Taggart, played by Mark McManus, stands at the center, a steady, determined investigator responsible not for patrol or pursuit, but for resolving the most serious crimes affecting ordinary lives.

Taggart centers its focus on the major investigation team. Murder is not solved by a single detective following a line of inquiry. It is resolved through coordinated effort. Witnesses must be identified and interviewed. Forensics examined and re-examined. Alibis checked. Pathologists consulted. Families managed. Evidence organized. Senior officers briefed. The senior investigating officer carries responsibility for all of it, ensuring the case continues to move forward even when progress slows and pressure increases. Murder investigations do not fade. They remain open, visible, and subject to scrutiny.

Time operates differently in these cases. Early decisions shape everything that follows. A missed witness, a poorly handled statement, a delay in securing evidence can redirect the entire investigation. As days pass, memory fades, leads weaken, and attention intensifies. The team must work against that erosion, preserving detail, maintaining momentum, and reassessing direction as new information emerges. Progress is not linear. It requires constant adjustment.

The series also emphasizes the emotional weight carried by the work. Robbery concerns property. Assault concerns violence. Murder concerns loss. In *Taggart*, detectives are not only pursuing a suspect. They are reconstructing the final movements of a life, building a case for someone who can no longer speak, and preparing it to withstand scrutiny in court. The responsibility extends beyond technical demands. It requires endurance, the ability to continue when progress slows, when repetition replaces momentum, and when outcomes remain uncertain.

Glasgow adds another dimension. The series demonstrates how policing is shaped by place. The crimes, the people, the neighborhoods, and the attitudes feel specific to the city. This sense of environment became a defining feature of later British crime drama, the recognition a detective series is not only about a crime, but about the setting in which it unfolds. In *Taggart*, Glasgow is not a backdrop. It is part of the investigation.

Like many major British crime series, *Taggart* extended into print. Five paperback novels by Peter Cave, based on original scripts by Glenn Chandler, were published by Mainstream during the show's early years. These included *Killer* (1985), based on the 1983 pilot, along with *Dead Giveaway* (1986), *Murder in Season* (1987), *Death Call* (1990), and *Evil Eye* (1992). A non-fiction volume, *Taggart Casebook: The First Ten Years* (1993), added behind-the-scenes material and case reconstructions. Together, these works reinforce the sense of a procedural world built around the demands of a murder squad.

In British police drama, *Taggart* represents the major investigation unit, responsible for the most serious crimes and for cases extending over weeks or longer. The work no longer centers on response or immediate action. It becomes sustained, structured, and subject to continuous review. The case does not end with an arrest. It must be built, maintained, and carried through to conclusion.

Pressure defines this level of policing. It comes from the case itself, from the expectation of results, and from the institution surrounding the investigation. Resources must be justified. Decisions must withstand scrutiny. Mistakes carry consequences beyond the immediate moment. Every step is examined, and every outcome measured.

At this scale, the work begins to attract attention from within the system as well as outside it. Oversight increases. Decisions are questioned. Conduct is reviewed. The investigation no longer belongs solely to those working it. Others begin to watch.

BETWEEN THE LINES—THE WATCHERS

Oversight emerges as police organizations grow in size and complexity. Authority comes under examination. Power is questioned. *Between the Lines* shifts attention away from criminals and toward the institution itself, exploring what happens when the police are required to investigate their own. Loyalty and accountability come into conflict, and the truth proves as difficult to uncover inside the organization as it is outside it.

The series centers on the Complaints Investigation Bureau, the division responsible for examining corruption, misconduct, and abuse of authority within the police. The shift alters the tone of the drama. In most crime series, the police pursue offenders. Here, the line is less certain. Suspects carry warrant cards. Witnesses are often officers. Investigators enter stations where they are not welcome and ask questions others would prefer left unasked.

This is a different form of policing. The work does not involve pursuit or controlled interviews with civilians. It involves experienced officers who understand procedure, understand how cases are constructed, and, at times, understand how to conceal what they have done. Every interview is measured. Every question carries weight. Every report affects not only a case, but careers and reputations.

Internal investigations are shaped as much by politics as by evidence. Senior officers consider scandal. Departments guard public image. Officers close ranks. Whistleblowers hesitate. Complaints investigators enter environments already resistant to scrutiny. Pressure operates at every level, influencing what is said, what is withheld, and what is recorded. Evidence does not stand alone. It moves through relationships, rank, and institutional interest.

The risk here is rarely physical. It is professional. A career can end as easily as a case can fail. Allegations carry weight before proof is established. Investigators must balance the need to establish facts with the knowledge that the process itself can damage reputations, whether misconduct is confirmed or not. The margin for error is narrow, requiring precision, restraint, and knowledge of how authority functions within the organization.

Between the Lines clearly demonstrates policing extends beyond enforcement. It requires the maintenance of standards. A force unwilling to examine itself risks losing public trust, and without that trust, its effectiveness erodes. Officers within the Complaints Investigation Bureau operate in a demanding space. They are part of the profession, yet required to stand apart from it. Loyalty exists, but not without limits.

The series reflects the climate of the late twentieth century, when policing in Britain faced increasing public scrutiny. Questions of corruption, misuse of authority, and accountability entered wider discussion. *Between the Lines* places those concerns at the center of its narrative, showing that the pressures of the job do not exist only on the street. They exist within the structure itself.

Like several other British police dramas, the series extended into print. Three original novels were published: *Breaking Point* by Diane Pascal, along with *The Chill Factor* and *Close Protection* by Tom McGregor. A dossier-style companion, *Tony Clark's Dossier* by Krystyna Zukowska, presented case-file material linked to the

Complaints Investigation Bureau. The decision to produce original stories rather than novelizations reflects the structure of the series, which often resembles a sequence of internal case files rather than a continuous narrative.

Within British police drama, *Between the Lines* represents oversight, the point at which the system examines itself. The work no longer focuses on crime alone, but on conduct, judgment, and the limits of authority. Decisions are reviewed. Actions are questioned. The institution becomes both subject and setting.

Under that scrutiny, the individual officer comes into sharper focus. Experience accumulates. Cases leave marks. Over time, the work shapes how a detective sees both the job and the people involved in it.

A TOUCH OF FROST—THE WEARY DETECTIVE

Time alters how a detective works. Years on the job bring knowledge, patience, and a sense of how cases develop. They also bring fatigue, frustration, and the knowledge not every case resolves cleanly. In *A Touch of Frost*, the seasoned detective takes shape, an officer who relies less on speed and more on persistence, less on theory and more on instinct formed over time.

Detective Inspector Frost, played by David Jason, is not a polished television figure. His coat is wrinkled, his desk cluttered, his reports late, and his superiors often close to losing patience with him. Yet he values something others overlook. The job revolves around people. Victims, witnesses, suspects, and the slow process of uncovering what actually happened. He listens. He watches. He asks questions others miss. And he cares, often more than is good for him.

That concern carries a cost. Frost does not separate himself easily from the work. Cases remain, not only in files, but in memory. The repetition of loss, of violence, of conversations with people at their worst, leaves its mark. The series does not emphasize this directly, but it is present in his weariness, in moments of irritation, and in the sense that the job is endured as much as performed.

A Touch of Frost is driven by experience. The earlier stages of policing—patrol, structure, specialist units, leadership, partnership, major investigation, internal oversight—have all passed through this point. Frost carries the accumulation. He knows procedure, but is not impressed by it. He understands bureaucracy, but does not admire it. He knows criminals lie, witnesses forget, and paperwork never ends. He recognizes when something does not fit, and understands that persistence, applied long enough, often exposes the truth.

The character originates in the novels of R. D. Wingfield, and the relationship between page and screen is notable. Six novels form the foundation: *Frost at Christmas* (1984), *A Touch of Frost* (1987), *Night Frost* (1992), *Hard Frost* (1995), *Winter Frost* (1999), and *A Killing Frost* (2008), the last published posthumously. The first three appeared before the television adaptation and established the character's tone. Later books followed during the series' run, maintaining a darker, less forgiving version of Frost than the television portrayal.

The series draws from these novels but often diverges in tone and structure. Jason's Frost retains the character's intelligence and compassion, but presents a warmer, more accessible figure. Even so, the novels were repeatedly republished with Jason's image, merging the literary and television versions in the public imagination.

After Wingfield's death, a series of prequel novels appeared under the name James Henry, a collaboration between James Gurbutt and Henry Sutton. These books—*First Frost*, *Fatal Frost*, *Morning Frost*, and *Frost at Midnight*—explore the earlier stages of the character's career, presenting a younger officer before the accumulated weight of experience becomes visible. Together, the original novels, the television series, and the prequels form one of the more extensive bodies of work associated with a British television detective.

Within British police drama, Frost represents the experienced investigator, an officer who understands both the strengths and the limitations of the system, and continues to work within it. He is not defined by speed or position. He conducts interviews, follows leads, and carries the weight of the job from one case to the next. The work is not abstract. It is personal, shaped by memory and repetition.

Experience brings patience, and patience often resolves cases speed cannot. The seasoned detective understands that most investigations develop slowly, shaped by persistence rather than sudden insight. But experience is not formed in isolation. It is shaped by conditions, by place, and by moments when the environment alters the work entirely.

FOYLE'S WAR—THE INVESTIGATOR

Context shapes the work of a detective. In times of crisis, it can alter the job completely. *Foyle's War* places the investigator in wartime Britain, where resources are limited, priorities shift, and the demands of national survival complicate the enforcement of the law. The result is a form of policing that must continually adapt to forces beyond its control.

Set during the Second World War, the series remains firmly a police drama rather than a battlefield narrative. Detective Chief Superintendent Christopher Foyle, played by Michael Kitchen, serves in Hastings, responsible for enforcing the law at a time when the law itself is under strain. Black market activity, espionage, theft, fraud, murder, desertion, and wartime profiteering all fall within his remit, many tied directly or indirectly to the war effort.

Foyle's War portrays policing when ordinary priorities no longer hold. Evidence disappears into classified channels. Suspects remain beyond reach because they are engaged in secret work. Cases are set aside because decisions made elsewhere determine that national interest outweighs prosecution. Foyle believes in the law, yet operates in a period when the law is sometimes treated as secondary to outcome.

The result is a different kind of investigation. Foyle does not simply solve crimes. He works within a system where truth may be concealed behind official secrecy, and where the legally correct resolution and the necessary wartime resolution do not always align. He stands at the point where conventional policing begins to intersect with intelligence work.

That intersection becomes more explicit as the series develops. Rather than concluding with victory, it continues into the postwar period. Foyle leaves traditional policing and moves into the emerging world of intelligence and security, where wartime alliances begin to fracture and new priorities take shape. The transition is handled with restraint, but its significance is clear. The skills of the detective—patience, observation, interviewing, and an deep insight into human behavior—transfer directly into intelligence work.

Within *The British TV Detective & Espionage Casebook*, this progression gives *Foyle's War* a distinctive position. It does not simply depict a wartime detective. It traces movement from one profession into another. Foyle begins with theft, fraud, and murder. He ends operating within a system defined by secrecy, intelligence, and national security. The series becomes a study in how closely those roles connect.

Unlike many of the series in this section, *Foyle's War* did not generate official tie-in novels. It did, however, produce a detailed non-fiction companion, *The Real History Behind Foyle's War*, written by Rod Green with a foreword by Anthony Horowitz. Published in 2006, the book examines the real wartime events and policies that informed the series, reinforcing its grounding in historical reality and its attention to the social conditions shaping each case.

Within British television drama, *Foyle's War* represents the investigator under pressure from history itself. The work is no longer defined solely by the crime or the suspect, but by forces operating beyond the immediate case. Decisions are shaped by circumstance as much as by evidence. Outcomes reflect not only what can be proven, but what can be permitted.

Under those conditions, the role of the detective shifts. Certainty becomes harder to establish. Resolution becomes conditional. The work continues, but it does so within limits set by events larger than any single investigation.

LUTHER—THE OBSESSIVE

The work does not always end when the case is closed, but detectives cannot always let it go. The case continues, carried forward into thought, memory, and daily life. In *Luther*, the job becomes more than a profession. It becomes a psychological burden. The detective is not simply solving crimes, but absorbing them, living with them, and being shaped by them. The line between the work and the man begins to disappear.

Detective Chief Inspector John Luther, played by Idris Elba, is not a controlled or composed television figure. He is brilliant, intuitive, and relentless, but also obsessive, impulsive, and often close to collapse. Where earlier detectives maintained some separation between work and life, he barely sustains one at all. Cases follow him home, into his sleep, into his relationships, and into his sense of identity. He does not leave the job. The job remains with him.

Luther centers on proximity rather than intensity. He works close to the edge of the crimes he investigates, relying on insight that approaches identification. He knows how offenders think, how they rationalize, how they act under pressure. Combined, those are the keys he uses to anticipate and respond, but they also places him in dangerous territory. The distance most detectives maintain begins to narrow. The work becomes personal, not by choice, but by necessity.

This stage in the progression draws together elements established in earlier series, but removes the safeguards. Procedure is understood, yet often resisted. Violent crime is confronted directly. Major investigations unfold under pressure, shaped by media attention, political oversight, and institutional constraint. Experience and instinct guide decisions, but without the distance that allows reflection. Everything operates at once, and nothing fully settles.

The series reflects a shift in how crime is presented. Earlier programs often focused on robbery, fraud, or contained acts of violence. *Luther* moves into darker territory, exploring serial offenders, psychological predators, and crimes that are both more intimate and more disturbing. The detective no longer works only to reconstruct events. He must anticipate behavior, enter patterns of thought, and engage with motives that are difficult to separate from the individuals who hold them.

That process carries consequences. The cost appears in fractured relationships, damaged trust, and an increasing sense of isolation. Luther's personal life does not run parallel to his work. It is shaped by it, often undermined by it. Colleagues question his methods. Superiors question his judgment. At times, he questions himself, though rarely for long. The drive to resolve the case overrides hesitation. The work continues.

At the center of the series is a tension between control and loss of control. Luther solves crimes through insight and persistence, yet his methods place him at risk of crossing the same boundaries he is meant to enforce. He acknowledges the rules. He also realizes when those rules may prevent an immediate result. That conflict defines the character. He operates within the system, but often at its limits.

Like several major British series, *Luther* extended into print, though in a manner consistent with its tone. Two novels by series creator Neil Cross—*Luther: The Calling* and *Luther: The Burning*—expand the character's background and psychological development. These are not adaptations, but prequels, exploring earlier cases, the breakdown of Luther's marriage, and his relationship with Ian Reed. Published in hardcover, they position the character within crime fiction as well as television, reinforcing the depth of the world he inhabits.

Within British television detective drama, Luther represents the point where the work is no longer contained by role, structure, or environment. It becomes internal. The detective carries it forward, case after case, without clear separation. Resolution does not restore balance. It creates space for the next investigation, and the next, each adding to what is already there.

For some detectives, the job remains external, defined by cases completed and reports filed. For others, it accumulates. It shapes perception, judgment, and response. In *Luther*, the accumulation is visible. The work leaves marks, not only on the case, but on the person conducting it.

The question is no longer how the detective works, but how long the detective can continue to work in that way.

NEW TRICKS—THE VETERANS

Experience does not disappear when a career ends. It remains in memory, in instinct, and in the cases left unresolved. *New Tricks* explores what happens when those investigations are reopened, and when the detectives who once worked them are given another opportunity to find the truth.

The premise is simple. A small unit is formed to re-examine unsolved crimes, staffed not by young officers building careers, but by retired detectives brought back for what they know. They are older, slower, and sometimes out of step with modern practice, yet they understand how criminals think and how investigations can fail. What they lack in pace, they replace with recognition.

New Tricks is built on memory. Unsolved cases do not disappear. They remain in files, in storage, and in the minds of the detectives who worked them. The returning officers are not only re-examining evidence. They are revisiting decisions, assumptions, and moments where something did not fit. The past is not fixed. It shifts as new information appears and as perspective changes.

The series also examines how policing evolves. The returning detectives come from a world defined by notebooks, informants, and direct questioning. The present they re-enter is shaped by databases, forensic advances, and procedural structure. The contrast drives the work. Experience identifies gaps technology does not recognize. Technology confirms patterns experience already suspects. Cases move when those approaches align.

Time introduces another variable. Witnesses reconsider what they saw. Relationships change. Motives once unclear begin to take shape. Distance can bring clarity, not because facts alter, but because context does. The returning detectives understand this. They approach older cases with patience, aware that answers sometimes emerge only when enough time has passed for the right questions to be asked.

The unit itself functions as a collection of perspectives shaped by different careers. Each officer carries a distinct approach, formed over years of work in different parts of the system. They argue, challenge one another, and test assumptions. Progress often comes through that friction, through the willingness to revisit conclusions others accepted. The work is not driven by urgency. It is driven by persistence and reconsideration.

A quieter recognition runs through the series. These detectives no longer need to prove themselves. The ambition that defined earlier stages of their careers has faded. What remains is a desire to resolve what was left incomplete. The cases are not abstract problems. They are unfinished business, tied to memory and, at times, to regret. Solving them offers resolution, not only for the investigation, but for the people who carried it.

Unlike many of the series in this section, *New Tricks* is not built on speed, confrontation, or institutional pressure. It operates at a different tempo. The work unfolds through conversation, reflection, and careful re-examination. The tension comes from whether the past can still be understood clearly enough to produce an answer.

Within British television detective drama, this represents a late stage of the profession. The work is no longer defined by position or authority, but by accumulated knowledge. Experience becomes the primary tool. Patterns repeat. Mistakes are recognized more quickly. What once required effort now comes through familiarity.

Retirement may end the formal career, but it does not end the work. Some cases remain open, not in the system, but in memory. They persist because they were never fully understood. Given the chance, the detective returns, not out of obligation, but because the question still remains.

CASE SUMMARY

Together, these series construct something resembling a professional blueprint of policing. Not perfect, and not official, but recognizable. From the officer answering the first call to the detective returning to an unresolved case years later, the work emerges as part of a continuous chain shaped by responsibility, experience, and change.

One pattern stands out. There is no single version of the detective. The role shifts with function, environment, and time. Some work at the point of first contact, establishing what happened before the investigation formally begins. Others build cases, assembling evidence and preparing it to withstand scrutiny. Some operate at speed, confronting violence as it unfolds. Others manage people, policy, and the direction of the work itself. Some reconstruct the most serious crimes, those who examine conduct within the profession, and those who carry knowledge accumulated over years. Some work under conditions where the law is shaped by larger events. Others absorb the psychological weight of the job until it becomes inseparable from how they think. And there are those who return after the career has ended, drawn back by cases that remain unresolved.

A clear progression emerges, tracing not only the career of a single officer, but the development of the profession as a whole. Policing begins as local and immediate, then becomes structured and procedural. Specialized roles emerge, leadership expands, and oversight follows. The work grows more visible, more complex, and, at times, more demanding on the individual. Over time, the profession turns back on itself, shaped by experience and by the accumulation of cases that resist simple resolution.

These series demonstrate, often without stating it directly, that policing depends less on individual brilliance than on persistence. Cases move forward because someone continues working. Because something does not fit and is not ignored. Because a question is asked again. Because a detail is remembered. The work rests on patience, repetition, and the steady accumulation of fact.

Alongside this professional tradition runs another current in British detective storytelling, one just as influential. It is the tradition of the investigator defined less by role than by identity. Education, class, intellect, and personality shape the work as much as procedure. Some of the most memorable figures in British crime fiction are not simply police officers. They are scholars, aristocrats, and amateurs, solving crimes not only as duty, but as expression of how they think.

To understand the British detective fully requires a shift in perspective. The station, the incident room, and the patrol car give way to different settings and different rhythms. Colleges, country houses, concert halls, libraries. Conversation replaces procedure. Observation takes a different form. The method remains, but the context changes.

From here, investigation moves beyond the station into a different world.

PART THREE

THE LITERARY DETECTIVES

These detectives began as fictional characters on the page and were later brought to television, often bringing their authors' worldview with them.

INTRODUCTION—THE MIND OF THE DETECTIVE

Working detectives are defined by their jobs. Literary detectives are defined by who they are. The distinction marks the shift from Part 2 to Part 3. The figures in the previous section carried warrant cards, answered to superiors, filed reports, and worked within structures shaping how cases progressed. Authority came from the role. Identity followed the profession. They were detectives because it was their occupation.

The literary detective operates on different terms. In British crime fiction and television, this figure is shaped less by role than by intellect, education, temperament, and background. Sometimes a police officer, sometimes not, but in either case effectiveness comes from the way the individual thinks. They notice different things. They ask different questions. They interpret behavior rather than simply recording it. Where the working detective resolves cases through process, the literary detective resolves them through insight.

The distinction extends beyond style. It reflects two approaches to the same problem. The professional begins with evidence and builds toward meaning. The literary detective often begins with meaning and works back toward evidence. Motive, behavior, and contradiction take precedence over sequence. The case becomes not just a series of events, but a pattern of choices requiring interpretation before resolution becomes possible.

This tradition runs deep in British storytelling. Long before television, detective fiction produced investigators defined as much by their minds as by their cases. They moved through country houses, Oxford colleges, London clubs, concert halls, and quiet villages. They quoted poetry, listened to opera, read history, and understood the unspoken rules governing class, status, and behavior. Crimes were resolved through attention. Who spoke too quickly. Who hesitated. Who remained silent. Who inherited money. Who had something to lose.

Television preserved this emphasis. These were not purely procedural dramas, but studies in perception. The cases matter, but the investigators matter more. The audience does not watch only to see who committed the crime. They watch to spend time with Morse, Campion, Dalgliesh, Lynley, and Gently. The crime provides structure. The detective provides substance.

Independence marks another distinction. Even within the police, these figures often stand slightly apart from the system. Rank exists, but does not define them. They may be educated men in a practical profession, aristocrats within democratic institutions, or poets working inside bureaucratic structures. Procedure is followed when required, but does not limit their thinking. A broader frame of reference, a sensitivity to nuance, and an approach not always aligned with formal expectations shape the work.

This independence allows movement across different social worlds. Morse belongs to Oxford, where knowledge and rivalry intersect. Campion inhabits the fading structures of aristocratic England. Dalgliesh moves among writers and artists, where language can conceal or reveal. Lynley moves between inherited privilege and professional responsibility. Each operates within a distinct environment, and reading that environment becomes essential to resolving the case.

Place, in these stories, is never incidental. It shapes behavior, expectation, and motive. A country house carries history and obligation. A college carries hierarchy and competition. A city carries anonymity and ambition. The literary detective reads these environments as carefully as people, recognizing context explains action as often as intention does.

These figures function as both investigator and interpreter. Through them, the audience sees how British society operates beneath the surface. Class influences behavior. Education shapes language. Ambition creates pressure. Resentment builds quietly over time. Motive grows from these conditions as much as from greed or anger. The task extends beyond determining what happened to interpreting why it occurred within a particular structure.

The rhythm of investigation changes as a result. Progress does not always move in a straight line. It circles, pauses, and returns. A conversation may matter more than a physical clue. A detail once dismissed becomes central. Resolution emerges through recognition rather than accumulation. The moment when everything aligns is less discovery than realization.

Insight carries consequence. A full reading of a crime includes its human cost, the relationships damaged, the ambitions undone, the private failures exposed. Distance may exist, but not detachment.

The role of the mind, not the presence or absence of a badge, shapes the investigation in this section. The question is not only how the case is solved, but how it is read. Not what is found, but what is recognized.

The working detective asks, “What can we prove?”

The literary detective asks, “What does this mean?”

Both lead to resolution. They begin from different assumptions, follow different paths, and arrive at the same point—an account of what happened, and why.

We begin with one of the most distinctly British figures of all, the gentleman amateur.

CAMPION—THE GENTLEMAN AMATEUR

Before procedure and rank defined the detective on screen, British fiction offered a different figure. Albert Campion belongs to that tradition, an investigator who operates without formal authority, relying instead on position, perception, and access. In *Campion*, crime is resolved not through official process, but through an awareness of society, class, and behavior. He is not a policeman. He is not paid to investigate. He carries no badge and answers to no superior. He is a gentleman amateur, and the term matters, not as a sign of inexperience, but as an indication of motive. He works because he chooses to.

Campion emerges from the world created by Margery Allingham, one of the central figures of the Golden Age. It is a setting shaped by country houses, old families, theatrical circles, and a social structure defined by class and connection. He moves easily within it, navigating between servants and aristocrats, shopkeepers and criminals, artists and officials. His polite manner and slightly vague public persona invite underestimation. That impression works in his favor. Beneath it sits constant attention, a habit of listening, and an ability to observe without drawing notice.

Campion's role here is social intelligence. His investigations depend less on evidence in the formal sense and more on reading behavior within a structured environment. Laboratories and interview rooms play little part. Instead, he interprets embarrassment, pride, inheritance, reputation, and the fear of exposure. These forces carry weight in a society where appearance matters and where disruption of status can have lasting consequences.

The television series, starring Peter Davison, captures this approach with precision. Produced in the late 1980s, it adapts Allingham's novels as period mysteries grounded in character and atmosphere rather than action. The pacing remains deliberate. Settings include country houses, theaters, and villages where routine conceals tension. The drama unfolds through conversation, implication, and the gradual exposure of motive. Violence exists, but rarely drives the story. The interest lies in how people behave when placed under quiet pressure.

The gentleman amateur occupies a distinct position within British storytelling. He moves through spaces closed to official inquiry. Questions take the form of conversation rather than interrogation. Invitations replace warrants. He comprehends the conventions governing behavior and notices when those conventions are strained or broken. Detection often depends on identifying discomfort, on recognizing when politeness conceals intention, and on discerning how individuals present themselves when something is at risk.

These stories depend on observation rather than action. Crimes often originate in earlier events, concealed relationships, or decisions made long before the investigation begins. Campion's strength lies in recognizing that motive rarely appears in simple form. Love, humiliation, jealousy, and fear operate beneath the surface. They do not appear in official records, yet they shape everything.

Another element defines his position. Campion operates between worlds. Not a police officer, yet frequently working alongside the police. He respects the law, but remains outside its procedures. He reflects a period in British detective fiction when the boundary between amateur and professional remained flexible. The solution may come from outside the system, even as the system ultimately enforces it.

Within the literary tradition, Campion represents a form of detection rooted in interpretation. He reads people as others read documents. He realizes how behavior shifts under pressure, how individuals protect reputation, and how truth hides behind convention. Because he is not seen as a threat, he is free to observe without interference.

The contrast with the working detective is clear. Where the professional relies on structure, Campion relies on access. Where the investigation builds through process, his develops through conversation and recognition. The setting may appear controlled, but the tensions beneath it are no less serious. A drawing room can conceal as much as any street.

This is one form of the literary detective. Another carries the same ease within society, but operates with official authority as well as personal insight. Inspector Alleyn enters that space, combining position with perception.

INSPECTOR ALLEYN—THE GENTLEMAN POLICEMAN

In British detective fiction, a distinction exists between the observer of society and the man who belongs within it. Chief Inspector Roderick Alleyn belongs. In *The Inspector Alleyn Mysteries*, drawn from the novels of Ngaio Marsh, he moves through aristocratic homes, theatrical circles, and artistic communities with ease, not as an outsider, but as someone entirely at home. What makes him unusual is the role he brings into that world. He is both gentleman and policeman, and his cases are shaped by that dual identity.

Played on television by Patrick Malahide, Alleyn is calm, educated, and self-contained, a man who rarely raises his voice and reveals little, yet misses almost nothing. The series, produced in the early 1990s, emphasizes atmosphere, character, and setting, echoing Campion while shifting the center of gravity. The stories unfold in country houses, theaters, film studios, and upper-class environments where manners matter and scandal can prove more damaging than violence. His advantage lies in familiarity. He is cognizant of how people speak, how they behave, what they fear, and what they attempt to conceal.

The television version places greater emphasis on procedure than Campion, but remains distant from the modern police procedural. Alleyn and his assistant, Inspector Fox, conduct interviews, observe behavior, and gradually assemble a picture of events. The pace remains deliberate. The focus rests on motive and character rather than forensic detail. Like many adaptations of Golden Age fiction, the series concerns itself less with systems and more with individuals under pressure.

What emerges is a figure defined not by performance, but by experience. Alleyn is not a gentleman playing at policing. He is a professional who has encountered violence directly. During the course of the stories, it becomes clear he served in the war and returned from it altered. The series does not name the condition, but what would now be recognized as post-traumatic stress informs the character. Control replaces display. Reserve replaces reaction. Emotional distance becomes a form of discipline rather than absence.

That experience separates him from the purely amateur figures of earlier fiction. He has seen what violence looks like without the filter of distance or decorum. He grasps what people are capable of doing. The knowledge gives weight to his manner. The series reveals this in small ways, a pause, a shift in tone, a moment of stillness when a case touches something familiar. The work is never abstract. It carries memory.

Alleyn occupies a transitional position within the literary detective tradition. He retains the ease of the gentleman, moving through a world shaped by class, reputation, and expectation, yet he operates with the authority of the police and the experience of a veteran. Social access, professional responsibility, and personal history combine in a single figure. He stands neither outside the system nor fully defined by it, but within a space where both influence the work.

The series captures this balance with precision. Malahide plays Alleyn as a man constantly observing, constantly evaluating, and always slightly removed from those around him. Polite but persistent. Sympathetic but exacting. Reputation carries force in his world, and that force often reveals motive. People act to protect standing, family, career, or identity. He recognizes the pattern because he has absorbed the structure behind it.

In contrast to Campion, who operates through access alone, Alleyn works with both access and authority. The distinction matters. He can enter a room by invitation, but he can also require answers. The investigation unfolds through a combination of conversation and obligation, where social ease and official responsibility reinforce one another.

His approach favors precision over display. There is little need for confrontation when insight provides leverage. The work advances through recognition, through identifying where behavior and circumstance diverge. And in the divergence lies the truth.

The emphasis now begins to shift again. Class and position recede, giving way to a different defining force. The next stage moves toward the detective shaped less by social world than by intellect itself.

INSPECTOR MORSE—THE SCHOLAR

Oxford runs on ideas, tradition, and ambition, and *Inspector Morse* is inseparable from that setting. Crime is rarely the whole story. It serves as an entry point. Beneath it lie academic rivalry, private disappointment, intellectual vanity, and emotional damage serious enough to lead to murder. Investigation becomes an act of interpretation, and in that process the detective takes shape as a scholar.

Played by John Thaw, Morse is one of the most fully realized figures in British television crime drama. He is experienced and respected, but rank does not define him. Education does. A classicist, an opera lover, a devotee of crosswords, he is a man whose mind is always at work, making connections, recognizing patterns, and detecting inconsistency. He drinks too much, falls in love too easily, and can be difficult to work with, yet he is often right because he empathizes with how people think and how they conceal what matters most.

Oxford becomes more than backdrop. Colleges, libraries, chapels, pubs, and quiet streets form the setting for stories rooted in intellectual life and the pressures accompanying it. Academic rivalry, professional jealousy, hidden relationships, financial strain, and damaged reputations drive many of the crimes. These are rarely acts of impulse. They develop over time, shaped by ambition, resentment, or fear of exposure. The motives become legible to a detective who understands the environment from which they arise.

The approach to detection reflects the setting. A case is not treated as a sequence of procedures, but as a problem requiring thought. Morse reads, listens to music, reflects, and allows ideas to develop. Theories form, collapse, and reform. Mistakes are frequent, but useful, each wrong turn narrowing the field of possibility. The path to the solution is rarely direct. It moves through contradiction, reinterpretation, and gradual recognition.

The partnership with Sergeant Lewis anchors the series. Morse provides the intellectual reach, the ability to sense the larger pattern before evidence fully confirms it. Lewis, played by Kevin Whately, provides steadiness, practical follow-through, and the steady advancement of the case. Together they represent two complementary modes of detection. Insight needs structure. Theory needs verification. One without the other remains incomplete.

The tone of the series is measured, reflective, and often touched with melancholy. Morse stands at a distance from the world around him. Intellectual fluency does not lead to personal ease. The result is a character defined as much by solitude as by intelligence, a man able to interpret the motives of others with precision while remaining less certain in his own life. That tension gives the series much of its emotional force.

Within the literary detective tradition, Morse represents intellectual authority. He carries a warrant card, but his influence comes from the ability to engage fully with the worlds he enters, academic, professional, and cultural. Like Campion and Alleyn, he moves through distinct layers of British society, though access comes through learning rather than inheritance. The distinction matters. This is not a figure born into ease, but one who has educated himself into it.

His method depends on interpretation, but not abstraction for its own sake. He does not think to avoid the work. He thinks in order to direct it. Motive sits at the center, and once motive becomes clear, the structure of the crime begins to resolve. The question is not only what occurred, but why it could occur in that particular environment, among those particular people.

Even so, intellect cannot complete an investigation by itself. Ideas have to be tested. Witnesses questioned. Evidence assembled. The finest theory remains useless until someone turns it into proof. That practical burden falls most often to the man beside him.

LEWIS—THE SERGEANT

For years, Robert Lewis stood slightly in the background, the steady presence beside a more complicated man. In *Lewis*, that position changes. No longer the assistant, he becomes the lead investigator, bringing with him the instincts of a career policeman shaped by experience rather than theory. Where Morse saw puzzles, Lewis sees people. His strength lies not in abstraction, but in his ability to predict how investigations will unfold in the real world, one interview, one decision, one detail at a time.

Played by Kevin Whately, the character is not an intellectual in the manner of Morse—no operatic references, no classical quotations, no sudden flashes of abstract insight. Instead, Lewis is experienced, patient, and has an instinctive grasp of human behavior. He listens carefully. He notices hesitation, shifts in tone, and small inconsistencies suggesting something is being withheld. The approach is quieter, steadier, and often more methodical.

The series reflects a more modern police environment than *Inspector Morse*. Procedure carries greater weight, forensic evidence is more prominent, and teamwork plays a larger role, yet the Oxford setting and intellectual atmosphere remain central. A new partnership forms with Sergeant James Hathaway, played by Laurence Fox, a figure markedly different from Morse. Hathaway is educated, analytical, and introspective, closer to Morse intellectually than Lewis himself. The dynamic reverses the earlier model. The former assistant becomes the senior officer, while the intellectual perspective shifts to the partner.

That partnership creates a balance between two forms of intelligence. Hathaway identifies patterns and explores ideas. Lewis understands people and the mechanics of police work. Together they form a complete investigative unit, combining intellect and experience in a way that both mirrors and develops the earlier relationship between Morse and Lewis.

Lewis represents an evolution. A working detective, defined in Part 2 terms by interviews, alibis, and procedure, gradually becomes a literary detective. Years of experience, first under Morse and later alongside Hathaway, reshape his approach. The focus broadens from proving a case to interpreting it. Motive, behavior, and consequence begin to carry as much weight as evidence.

Personal history also informs the development. Loss and experience bring a depth of empathy influencing how cases are approached. Grief, regret, and disappointment are not abstract concepts. They are lived realities, and this awareness allows motives to be understood in ways not immediately apparent.

Within the literary detective tradition, Lewis represents practical wisdom. He may not be the most formally educated person in the room, and he may not be the quickest to form a theory, but he is intimate with how investigations function and how individuals respond under pressure. He is steady where others are mercurial, patient where others are impulsive, and perceptive in a manner developed over time rather than appearing fully formed.

Intellect defines Morse. Experience defines Lewis. The progression from one to the other traces a movement from theory toward judgment, from abstraction toward application. It does not reject intellect, but integrates it into a broader interpretation of the work.

The path does not begin at this level of confidence. Every experienced detective was once a beginner, uncertain, untested, and still learning what the job requires.

ENDEAVOUR—THE YOUNG DETECTIVE

Every accomplished detective begins in uncertainty, learning the job through experience rather than assumption. *Endeavour* returns to that beginning. Set in the 1960s, the series introduces a young Morse at the start of his career, a man with a remarkable mind but little practical grounding. The confidence and authority seen later have not yet formed. What emerges instead is the process through which a detective takes shape.

The series makes clear that ability alone is not enough. Skill develops through experience, through mentorship, through error, and through cases that resist resolution. Early in his career, Morse relies heavily on instinct and intellect, but those qualities do not always guide him safely. He misjudges people, pushes too far, and at times fails to recognize the consequences of his decisions. Each mistake leaves an impression, refining judgment and forcing a balance between insight and restraint.

At the center of this process stands Detective Inspector Fred Thursday, played by Roger Allam. Thursday represents the working detective in its most grounded form, practical, experienced, and shaped by years on the job. He has little interest in abstraction, yet understands people, understands criminals, and understands how investigations succeed or fail. His presence provides structure. He teaches Morse when to act, when to hold back, and how to manage pressure without losing control.

The Oxford of *Endeavour* differs from the one seen later in *Inspector Morse*. Tradition remains, but change is evident. Youth culture, shifting class structures, and new forms of crime begin to alter the environment. Morse understands the academic world through education, yet does not fully belong within it. As a young detective, he does not entirely belong within the police either. This sense of displacement becomes central. He moves between environments without settling comfortably in either, observing both without complete attachment.

The cases reflect this instability. They are layered, shaped by changing social conditions, and often resist straightforward explanation. Morse identifies patterns others miss, making intuitive connections that frequently prove correct. The series does not present this ability as effortless. Insight comes with strain. Long hours, isolation, and responsibility begin to shape him early. The distance associated with the older Morse is already visible, not fully formed, but emerging.

Becoming a detective involves more than learning technique. It requires learning how to carry the work. Morse encounters not only crime, but its consequences, for victims, for families, and for himself—moments when the human cost becomes difficult to ignore. These moments do not weaken him. They deepen his awareness, shaping how he approaches both suspects and situations.

Within the literary detective tradition, *Endeavour* represents potential. Intellectual capacity is present, but untempered. Instinct leads, sometimes correctly, sometimes not. Experience, provided through mentorship and exposure, begins to shape it into something more reliable. The series becomes an education in judgment, showing how intellect and experience must eventually converge.

In that sense, *Endeavour* forms a bridge between the two worlds explored in this book. Thursday embodies experience, discipline, and practical knowledge. Morse embodies intellect, perception, and curiosity. Their partnership demonstrates how these approaches combine. Intelligence without experience risks error. Experience without imagination risks limitation. Effective detection requires both.

Character develops alongside skill. A sense of justice, sympathy for outsiders, resistance to misplaced authority, and a willingness to question assumptions all begin to take shape. These qualities do not appear fully formed. They develop through confrontation, failure, and reflection. The young detective is not only learning how to solve cases, but what kind of detective he will become.

Progress is uneven. Growth comes through both success and failure. Over time, what emerges is not simply greater ability, but greater control, and a construction ideal of both possibility and limitation.

From that foundation, another element begins to take precedence. Not intellect alone, and not experience alone, but a sense of judgment grounded in principle.

INSPECTOR GEORGE GENTLY—THE MORAL CENTER

Some detectives rely on intellect. Others rely on experience. George Gently is defined by principle. In *Inspector George Gently*, the central question extends beyond who committed the crime to what is right, what is wrong, and what follows when those lines begin to blur. He works in a changing Britain, yet his sense of justice remains fixed.

The television version diverges in tone from the character created by Alan Hunter. In the novels, Gently is quieter, more traditional. On screen, Martin Shaw plays him with a harder edge, shaped by exposure to violence, corruption, and the more troubling aspects of human behavior. Patience for dishonesty, particularly within the police, has worn thin. The shift introduces a sharper internal tension. He is a good policeman operating at a time when both policing and society are in transition.

The setting intensifies the conflict. The 1960s bring social upheaval, shifting class structures, emerging youth culture, and growing skepticism toward authority. Within the police, questions of corruption, brutality, and misuse of power become harder to ignore. Gently belongs to an earlier framework, grounded in the belief that the law should apply equally and that the role of a detective is to establish the truth rather than settle for convenience.

That belief is tested repeatedly. He works alongside officers willing to cut corners, accept favors, or overlook misconduct. Refusal to follow that path isolates him. Promotions pass by. Relationships strain. Progress slows. The work continues nonetheless, guided by a standard that does not adjust to circumstance. In this environment, integrity is not abstract. It is a daily decision, often made without support.

The series recognizes that moral clarity does not mean simplicity. Cases present competing claims, partial truths, and situations where legal outcome and just outcome do not align. Gently does not avoid the tension. He works through it, weighing consequence alongside fact. The process may take longer, but it remains deliberate. The aim is not only to resolve the case, but to do so without weakening the principles behind the work.

His relationship with Detective Sergeant John Bacchus provides the clearest expression of this approach. Bacchus is ambitious, uncertain, and at times willing to bend rules to achieve results. Gently serves as mentor, though the lesson differs from earlier pairings. The focus is not on how to think, but on how to remain steady under pressure without losing direction. Procedure can be taught. Judgment develops through example.

Within the literary detective tradition, Gently represents the detective as conscience. He does not depend on intellectual display or social position. Authority comes from consistency, from an unwillingness to compromise essential principles even when the cost is personal. Victims matter. Truth matters. The legitimacy of the law rests on how it is applied.

A connection to earlier forms of British television policing remains. Shaw's performance carries an echo of his work in *The Professionals*, a series defined by speed and force. Here, the emphasis shifts. The pace slows. Decisions are considered. The character suggests a man who has seen the consequences of urgency unchecked and chosen a different path, guided by restraint rather than reaction.

Gently's method is neither intellectual in the manner of Morse nor experiential in the manner of Lewis alone. It is evaluative. Each decision is measured against a standard not easily altered. The work becomes less about solving the case quickly and more about resolving it correctly.

He does not rely on rank or brilliance to establish authority. He relies on consistency, on a refusal to accept compromise where it matters most. In doing so, he defines a standard against which others can be measured.

From this point, the focus begins to shift inward. The question is no longer how the detective acts, but how the detective reflects.

DALGLIESH—THE POET

Quiet authority defines certain detectives. They do not need to raise their voices to be heard. Adam Dalgliesh stands among them. In the television adaptations of P. D. James's novels, he moves through investigations with a deliberate, measured presence, revealing little while observing closely. A senior police officer and a published poet, he approaches crime not simply as an act, but as the final expression of something developing over time beneath the surface.

Dalgliesh originates in a body of work where character and motive take precedence over pace. These are not fast-moving procedurals. They unfold gradually, attentive to emotional detail and the inner lives of those connected to the crime. The television adaptations preserve this tone. Investigation becomes a process of listening, observing, and reflecting, allowing meaning to emerge rather than forcing it into view.

Dalgliesh works through reflection, filtering intellect and principle before they are applied. As a poet, he attends to language, to silence, and to the spaces between what is said and what is meant. This attention carries into his work. He notices hesitation, tone, and unguarded moments. Motive rarely appears directly. It reveals itself through pattern and implication.

His method remains understated. He does not rush or dominate conversation. Questions are posed quietly, often with the appearance of simplicity, and responses unfold at their own pace. In this space, people speak more freely than they might under pressure. The truth is not forced. It surfaces. The approach requires patience and a tolerance for uncertainty as the case develops.

Observation does not end with others, but turns inward. Dalgliesh weighs what he sees, considering not only evidence, but meaning. Crime becomes part of a broader human context, shaped by loss, ambition, resentment, and fear. The act cannot be separated from the life that produces it.

Rank introduces another layer. As a Commander, he carries authority and responsibility, yet remains directly involved in the investigation. Files are read with care. Interviews are conducted with precision. Decisions reflect consequence as well as outcome. Leadership does not remove him from the work. It places him where judgment must be exercised with restraint.

The visual world reinforces this sensibility. Settings are often enclosed and self-contained, private hospitals, publishing houses, coastal communities, and institutions where individuals live in close proximity and tension builds gradually. These environments function as contained systems. Each relationship carries weight. Each silence suggests something withheld. Moving through them requires sensitivity rather than force.

Within the literary detective tradition, Dalgliesh represents introspection. Insight comes through attention rather than display. Complexity is not reduced. It is acknowledged and worked through.

A sense of solitude accompanies this perspective. Like Morse, he stands slightly apart, though the distance takes a different form. Where Morse turns outward, Dalgliesh turns inward. Poetry provides a way to order experience, to give shape to what is observed. The distance sharpens involvement rather than diminishing it.

Each case carries the weight of a longer narrative. The crime marks an ending, but meaning lies in what precedes it, the relationships, decisions, and pressures leading to that point. His task is to trace that progression and place the act within it.

Detection, in this form, becomes interpretation. The answer is not simply found. It is recognized.

From here, the focus shifts again, toward a detective navigating identity within a structure shaped by class and expectation.

INSPECTOR LYNLEY MYSTERIES—THE ARISTOCRAT DETECTIVE

Class shapes British life in ways both visible and subtle, and few detectives carry that influence as directly as Thomas Lynley. In *The Inspector Lynley Mysteries*, he serves as both senior police officer and earl, a man whose authority comes from two distinct sources. One is earned through the profession. The other arrives with birth. The tension between them drives both character and series.

At the center stands the partnership between Lynley and Detective Sergeant Barbara Havers, played by Sharon Small. Havers comes from a working-class background, direct in manner and skeptical of authority, especially the kind Lynley represents. To her, he embodies privilege, someone who has not needed to struggle for position or recognition, someone who could leave policing and return to a life defined by title and wealth. From his perspective, she represents the practical reality of the job, experience, instinct, and an unfiltered recognition of how people live beyond influence and status.

The contrast does not resolve easily. Trust develops through friction, disagreement, and shared work rather than immediate alignment. Each exposes the limits of the other. Lynley must demonstrate that education and rank do not define his ability.

Havers must recognize that control and discipline can serve the investigation as effectively as instinct. Their effectiveness grows from tension rather than harmony.

The series uses this dynamic to examine class without softening its edges. Policing presents itself as a merit-based profession, advancement tied to performance rather than background. Lynley enters carrying advantages that complicate that ideal. Status, wealth, and influence follow him into the job. Whether those elements weaken or strengthen his position remains an open question, answered only through conduct.

Many cases return him to familiar ground, the upper classes, old families, inherited wealth, and long-standing networks of influence. Access comes easily. So does recognition. Like earlier figures in this tradition, he holds the key to the codes governing behavior in these environments. Discretion, reputation, and quiet power operate beneath the surface. Obligation is the difference. He cannot observe from a distance. He represents the law, and action follows discernment.

That obligation produces sustained conflict. Belonging and responsibility do not align. Investigating his own social world places him in a position where loyalty and duty intersect. Choosing the latter carries consequences, not only in strained relationships, but in how he is aware of himself. The role requires adjustment, not of status, but of identity.

The series makes clear that balance is not maintained automatically. Authority cannot be assumed. It must be established in the presence of those prepared to challenge it. Respect emerges gradually, built through decisions rather than position. Over time, visible markers of class begin to recede, replaced by consistency of action.

Havers remains central to that shift. She questions, resists, and refuses to defer. Her presence demands clarity. In response, Lynley acknowledges her ability and supports her standing within the system, even when it brings conflict with senior officers. Their partnership becomes essential, not because differences disappear, but because both learn to work within them.

Within the literary detective tradition, Lynley represents the aristocrat under pressure. Education, position, and inherited responsibility remain part of his background, but they no longer define the work. What matters is accountability, to the law, to colleagues, and to those affected by the crime. Duty becomes immediate rather than abstract.

With time, class loses its central hold. Experience, judgment, and consequence reshape the individual. The title remains, but it carries less weight than the role he chooses to fulfill.

From here, the focus moves toward what remains after identity has been tested and altered, when the work itself becomes the defining force.

LYNLEY—THE ARISTOCRAT REBORN

Time reshapes detectives as surely as it reshapes the world around them. In this later phase, Lynley is no longer defined primarily by aristocracy, but by responsibility. The title remains, yet it carries less weight. What matters now is the work, the cases, and the burden of leadership within a modern investigative environment.

Earlier, the central question asked whether an aristocrat could function within a profession grounded in merit, discipline, and practical ability. Much of the drama emerged from that tension, particularly in the relationship with Barbara Havers, whose skepticism toward privilege proved both justified and necessary. In this later form, the question recedes. The world has shifted, and the character has adjusted with it. Class persists, but no longer drives the narrative.

The setting reflects this change. Contemporary policing places greater emphasis on scale, coordination, and accountability. Investigations expand. Scrutiny arrives quickly. Decisions carry wider consequences. Within this structure, Lynley operates as a senior investigator whose authority depends on judgment rather than assumption.

Leadership moves to the center. Responsibility extends beyond solving a case to directing others, balancing competing pressures, and maintaining control over complex investigations. The role requires distance as well as involvement, an ability to see the larger structure while remaining attentive to detail. It is a quieter form of detection, less visible, but no less demanding.

The shift alters the nature of certainty. Earlier, resolution came through full awareness, motive identified, events reconstructed, the case brought to a clear conclusion. At a senior level, clarity is rarely complete. Decisions must be made before every element is known, and those decisions extend beyond a single case. Judgment replaces certainty as the defining skill.

The transition carries cost. Movement into command changes the relationship to the work. Direct engagement gives way, in part, to oversight. Information arrives filtered, summarized, structured. Something is gained in scope, yet immediacy diminishes. Maintaining connection to the human element becomes an effort rather than a given. Effective leaders recognize this and compensate for it.

The relationship with Havers reflects that evolution. Earlier tension rooted in class difference gives way to professional trust. Experience replaces suspicion. Each understands the other's approach and limitations. The partnership no longer depends on contrast, but on reliability. Loyalty becomes a working principle rather than a point of conflict.

Within the structure of this book, Lynley occupies a transitional position. Part 3 has examined detectives defined by identity, education, class, morality, and personality. Here, the emphasis begins to move toward system, procedure, and institutional responsibility. Lynley stands between those worlds, emerging from the literary tradition while operating within the framework of modern policing.

In that position, he represents the detective as leader. Background remains part of the foundation, but it no longer determines effectiveness. What matters is the ability to guide an investigation, to make decisions under pressure, and to accept responsibility for the outcome. Authority is measured through action.

The progression echoes developments seen earlier in the profession. Advancement alters the nature of the work. Less time is spent conducting interviews. More time is spent directing others, assessing information, and managing consequence. The role becomes less personal and more structural, though the weight of individual decisions remains.

The transformation is gradual but clear. Identity recedes. Function takes its place. The detective becomes part of a larger system, shaped by it and responsible to it.

From here, the perspective widens, drawing together the forms of thought, identity, and responsibility that define the literary detective.

CASE SUMMARY

Background, rank, and temperament differ, but the individuals in this section share a consistent approach. Crime is resolved not only through procedure, but through interpretation. Campion reads social behavior. Alleyn moves within society while carrying the authority of the law. Morse interprets intellect and ambition. Lewis understands people and the practical realities of investigation. Endeavour shows how intellect becomes experience. Gently measures right and wrong. Dalgliesh attends to the inner life. Lynley balances class, responsibility, and leadership. Each approaches crime from a different angle, yet all depend on thought as much as action.

British television has long presented detectives as complete individuals rather than functional roles. Education, background, and temperament shape how each operates. Morse turns to language and music. Dalgliesh to reflection. Campion to social fluency. Lynley to the tension between inheritance and duty. Gently to principle. These qualities are not decorative. They are operational. The mind becomes the primary instrument of detection.

Setting reinforces this approach. Each investigator is rooted in a distinct environment. Oxford for Morse and Lewis. Country houses and theatrical circles for Campion and Alleyn. The industrial North for Gently. Enclosed institutions and private communities for Dalgliesh. The intersection of class and profession for Lynley. These worlds do more than provide context. They generate motive. Crime grows from jealousy, ambition, resentment, fear, or the need to protect reputation. Reading the environment becomes essential to interpreting the act.

In these stories, detection becomes interpretation. Evidence exists, but does not explain itself. It must be read, placed within a broader pattern, and connected to human intention. Resolution emerges through recognition, the moment when separate elements align and meaning becomes clear. This moment defines the literary detective.

The investigative process extends beyond method. It becomes intellectual and emotional, shaped by perception as much as procedure. Authority may come from the institution, yet resolution often depends on insight, on recognizing absence, concealment, and contradiction.

This emphasis on the individual mind offers both strength and limitation. It allows depth and nuance, but depends on perspective that cannot always scale. As cases expand in scope and the world surrounding them becomes more interconnected, the solitary or semi-solitary thinker begins to give way to something broader.

Part 2 showed how the job operates. Part 3 shows how the mind engages with it. Crime originates in human behavior, and recognizing behavior remains essential. The question now is how this insight adapts as the scale of investigation expands.

The profession does not remain static. By the late twentieth century, the detective story shifts. Forensic science advances. Investigations expand. Media attention intensifies. Oversight increases. The individual detective, whether sergeant or scholar, no longer stands alone. The incident room, the forensic lab, the analyst, the major case team—detection becomes system.

PART FOUR

THE MODERN ERA

These shows changed the detective from a professional solving cases into a flawed human being struggling with the job.

INTRODUCTION—THE AGE OF METHOD

The modern detective no longer works alone. This marks one of the most significant changes in British television crime drama from the late twentieth century onward. The solitary figure, whether uniform constable, CID investigator, or intellectual outsider, gives way to something larger. Investigation becomes organized, structured, and increasingly complex. The detective remains central, but no longer stands alone. The work expands outward, drawing in systems, specialists, and processes reshaping how cases are read and resolved.

This evolution reflects changes in policing itself. Major investigations expand in scale, at times involving dozens of officers working different aspects of the same case. Forensic science moves from support to central function, capable of identifying, confirming, and at times contradicting investigative assumptions. Computers alter how information is stored, retrieved, and connected, allowing patterns to emerge across time and geography. Media coverage becomes constant, placing cases under immediate public scrutiny. Oversight increases, and police officers find themselves examined as closely as the crimes they investigate.

The work does not become simpler. It becomes broader, more visible, and more accountable.

Television responds by altering narrative structure. The incident room replaces the lone office as the primary setting. Walls covered with photographs, timelines, and reports become a visual representation of thought in progress. Evidence no longer sits in a single file. It is distributed across a system requiring coordination to function. Teams pursue parallel lines of inquiry. One group handles witnesses. Another follows suspects. Others manage intelligence, forensic results, and background information. The narrative shifts from individual action to the movement of a case through a system.

This change brings new figures into focus. Scientists, analysts, pathologists, psychologists, and media officers become integral to the process. Each contributes a specific form of knowledge. Each operates within defined limits. The challenge lies not only in gathering information, but in integrating it. A forensic result may suggest one direction. A witness statement another. Intelligence a third. The task is to reconcile these elements, determining what holds, what fails, and how each fits within the larger picture.

As a result, the role of the detective changes. No longer defined solely by instinct or individual insight, the modern investigator becomes a coordinator, a decision-maker, and often a leader. The Senior Investigating Officer directs the case, allocating resources, setting priorities, and determining strategy. Decisions carry immediate consequences. A misjudgment can delay progress, misdirect effort, or allow opportunity to pass. Authority is expressed not only through action, but through the ability to manage complexity.

This structure also introduces new pressures. Time matters not only in solving the case, but in managing expectation. Media attention shapes perception before conclusions are reached.

Internal review examines decisions while the investigation remains active. The detective operates within multiple timelines, the pace of the case, the pace of public attention, and the pace of institutional response.

The series in this section trace that development from multiple angles. *Prime Suspect* establishes the Senior Investigating Officer at the center of large-scale inquiry, where leadership influences outcome as much as evidence. *Cracker* introduces psychological profiling, shifting attention toward the inner life of the offender. *Silent Witness* places forensic science at the center of the investigative process. *Line of Duty* examines the system itself, where procedure and accountability become subjects of investigation. *Broadchurch* explores the impact of public scrutiny on case and community. *Happy Valley* returns to the frontline, showing how these pressures affect the individual officer. *Unforgotten* engages with time, demonstrating how cases evolve across years. *Vera* and *Shetland* emphasize the role of place within a structured system. *The Fall* examines the relationship between investigator and offender in psychological terms. *Grace* connects past and present, combining traditional methods with modern techniques. *Inspector Ellis* brings these elements together, presenting a detective navigating the full scope of the contemporary investigative landscape.

What emerges from these portrayals is a conception of investigation as coordinated effort shaped by procedure, technology, and collaboration. The solution does not come from a single insight, but from alignment. Evidence is tested against analysis. Analysis against experience. Experience against oversight. The process advances through interaction.

The detective remains essential, but the nature of that importance changes. The modern investigator does not stand apart from the system. He operates within it, directing, interpreting, and responding to the flow of information moving through multiple channels. The work is no longer defined by isolation, but by integration.

The modern era does not replace earlier forms of detection. It builds on them. Instinct remains. Observation remains. Experience remains. What changes is the environment in which those qualities operate, and the scale at which they must function.

TENNISON—THE MAKING OF THE MODERN DETECTIVE

Beginning the modern era with *Tennison* may seem unconventional. The series functions as a prequel to *Prime Suspect*, yet chronology is not the organizing principle here. This section follows professional development, focusing on what each series reveals about the work itself. *Tennison* matters because it shows the starting point, the conditions from which the modern detective emerges.

Played by Stefanie Martini, the young Jane Tennison enters a police force still governed by older habits. The environment is male-dominated, hierarchical, and resistant to change. Authority operates as much through personality as through rank. Procedure lacks consistency. Evidence handling varies from case to case. Advancement depends on acceptance within the culture as much as on demonstrated ability. This is not yet the structured, accountable system seen later. It is something looser, less defined, and more dependent on individual discretion. It captures a moment of transition rather than stability.

Tennison is ambitious, perceptive, and determined, yet her progress is neither smooth nor guaranteed. She encounters resistance at every level, open skepticism from colleagues, exclusion from decision-making, and a persistent need to justify her presence. Competence alone does not secure position. It must be demonstrated repeatedly under scrutiny. This pressure shapes her approach. She learns quickly, adapts where necessary, and develops a resilience that becomes central to her effectiveness.

Then the work itself begins to change. Cases increase in complexity, no longer contained within simple lines of inquiry. Multiple suspects, conflicting statements, and expanding timelines require coordination. The investigation becomes something that must be managed, not simply pursued. Information accumulates at a pace that demands structure. Decisions must be made about what to follow, what to set aside, and how to allocate limited resources.

Within this environment, Tennison begins to understand that detection involves more than identifying a suspect. It requires control. Evidence must be handled consistently. Information must be organized. Interviews must be conducted with purpose rather than instinct alone. The idea of a directed investigation starts to take form, even if the system supporting it remains incomplete. She operates in the space between older methods and emerging practice, learning to impose order where little exists.

It also highlights the role of observation at a practical level. Tennison notices gaps others ignore, inconsistencies in statements, patterns of behavior that suggest more than surface detail reveals. These instincts remain essential, but they are increasingly tied to a broader process. Insight must lead somewhere. It must be followed, tested, and integrated into the developing case. The transition from intuition to method begins here.

The cost of the work becomes visible early. Professional demands narrow personal life. Time is consumed by the job. Relationships strain or fall away. The role begins to shape identity, not through choice, but through accumulation. Each case adds weight. Each decision leaves an impression. The separation between personal and professional becomes harder to maintain.

This is not yet the fully realized burden seen in later series, but its foundation is clear.

An additional dimension appears in the novels written by Lynda La Plante. Beginning with *Tennison* (2015), she developed a sequence including *Hidden Killers*, *Good Friday*, *Murder Mile*, *The Dirty Dozen*, *Blunt Force*, *Unholy Murder*, *Dark Rooms*, *Taste of Blood*, and *Whole Life Sentence*. These books extend Tennison's early career, exploring institutional resistance, procedural development, and the gradual shaping of a detective learning how the job functions in practice. They read less as adaptations and more as case histories, grounded in the same evolving landscape presented on screen.

What *Tennison* ultimately establishes is a point of origin. Traditional policing does not disappear, but it begins to give way to something more structured and accountable. Instinct and experience remain valuable, yet they no longer carry an investigation on their own. The work demands coordination, consistency, and control. The detective must not only pursue the case, but manage it.

From this foundation, the modern form takes shape. Leadership becomes central. The investigation expands. The system begins to define the work.

The development finds its full expression in the figure Tennison becomes

PRIME SUSPECT—THE MODERN SENIOR INVESTIGATIONG OFFICER

When *Prime Suspect* aired in 1991, it did more than introduce a new detective. It altered the structure of the role within British television drama. The focus moved away from the individual investigator working toward a solution and toward the figure responsible for directing the entire process.

Detective Chief Inspector Jane Tennison, played by Helen Mirren, operates as the Senior Investigating Officer. The distinction matters. She does not work alongside a partner or pursue leads independently. She leads the inquiry. Tasks are assigned. Resources are allocated. Evidence is evaluated within a broader framework. Progress depends on coordination rather than individual initiative. The investigation becomes something managed as well as solved.

This shift changes the nature of detection. A case is no longer defined by the insights of a single figure, but by the movement of information through a structured system. Lines of inquiry develop in parallel. Decisions must be made about priority, direction, and timing. Tennison's role requires constant assessment, determining which lead advances the case and which diverts it. Authority is expressed through judgment applied under pressure.

The series also introduces a level of institutional realism that proves both influential and difficult to ignore. Sexism within the police force is not background detail. It shapes the investigation itself. Tennison faces resistance from colleagues who question her authority, challenge her decisions, and seek to undermine her position. Control of the case must be asserted repeatedly. Leadership is not granted. It is enforced.

This conflict operates at multiple levels. Superiors apply pressure from above, concerned with outcomes and public perception. Subordinates resist direction, testing limits and challenging authority. The investigation proceeds within an environment where the legitimacy of command remains in question. Tennison must establish control while simultaneously managing the case. The two cannot be separated.

The series also redefines the portrayal of women in detective drama. Tennison is neither symbolic nor exceptional in a simplified sense. She is competent, determined, and often correct, yet she works within a structure not designed to support her. The pressure is continuous. Professional decisions carry personal consequences. Relationships narrow. Isolation increases. The role demands commitment that leaves little space for anything outside it.

Visually, the series establishes the language of the modern investigation. The incident room becomes central. Walls filled with photographs, timelines, and reports reflect the scale and complexity of the case. Information is no longer contained. It is displayed, organized, and constantly revised. Teams divide responsibility. Witnesses are interviewed by one group, suspects pursued by another, forensic results analyzed elsewhere. The investigation becomes visible as a process.

Procedure gains equal weight with instinct. Forensic evidence informs direction. Statements are cross-checked. Timelines are constructed and reconstructed. Each element contributes to a larger framework requiring coordination to function. The role of the detective shifts from discovering the answer to directing the process through which the answer emerges.

Leadership carries consequence. Authority isolates. Responsibility accumulates. Every decision affects the course of the investigation and the people working within it. Errors are amplified by scale. Success depends not only on solving the case, but on managing the conditions under which it is solved. Tennison's personal life narrows as the demands of the role expand. Command is presented not as status, but as burden.

Lynda La Plante extended Tennison's story through a series of novels, including *Prime Suspect*, *Prime Suspect 2: A Face in the Crowd*, and *Prime Suspect 3: Silent Victims*. Written by the creator of the series, these books follow the same structure, focusing on major investigations and Tennison's responsibility for directing them. They read as extensions of her professional life, reinforcing the idea the work centers on managing complexity as much as resolving crime.

What *Prime Suspect* establishes is a new definition of the detective. Leadership, organization, and decision-making replace individual insight as the primary drivers of the investigation. The work no longer belongs to a single figure. It moves through a system, shaped by procedure and sustained by coordination.

From this point, attention begins to shift again, away from structure and toward the mind of the offender.

CRACKER—THE PSYCHOLOGICAL PROFILER

Often cases resist explanation through evidence alone. When *Cracker* arrived in the early 1990s, it introduced a different kind of specialist into the investigative process, one who does not collect evidence, make arrests, or direct an incident room. The focus turns toward interpretation. Crime is no longer treated only as an event to reconstruct, but as behavior requiring empathetic insight.

Dr. Edward Fitz Fitzgerald, played by Robbie Coltrane, operates outside formal police authority. His contribution lies in insight rather than procedure. He studies language, impulse, contradiction, and compulsion, examining crimes not only for what occurred, but for what they reveal about the person responsible. In cases driven by obsession, repetition, or psychological disturbance, this perspective becomes essential. Evidence can establish events. It cannot always explain motive. Fitz works within that gap.

The structure of the series reflects this shift. The identity of the offender is often revealed early, redirecting attention away from discovery and toward interpretation. The question changes. Not who committed the crime, but what kind of person would commit it, and what that suggests about future behavior. Fitz analyzes patterns, reconstructs internal logic, and uses the knowledge gained to guide the investigation, provoke admissions, or anticipate escalation. The case develops through interpretation as much as procedure.

This approach depends on a different kind of observation. Small details carry disproportionate weight. The way a suspect speaks. What is avoided. How a story is constructed. Where emotion appears or fails to appear. Each element becomes part of the evidentiary field. Fitz listens for imbalance, contradiction, and displacement. A casual remark may matter more than a formal statement. A repeated behavior may reveal more than a single act. The investigation begins to resemble psychological mapping, where actions are placed within a framework of thought and impulse.

Interviews change accordingly. They are no longer limited to establishing timelines or confirming facts. They become confrontational, strategic, and deliberately unsettling. Fitz pushes, provokes, and destabilizes, forcing suspects to confront aspects of themselves they would prefer to conceal. The objective is not only to gather information, but to create conditions in which maintaining a lie becomes increasingly difficult. The line between analysis and manipulation remains intentionally thin.

The method carries risk. Fitz is perceptive, but unstable, a gambler, a drinker, and a man whose private life mirrors the disorder he studies. His ability to understand offenders comes at a cost. He recognizes patterns because he can approach them from the inside. That proximity creates vulnerability. Insight and instability exist side by side. The skill enabling interpretation also exposes him to what he interprets.

The boundary between observer and subject becomes uncertain. Fitz studies offenders, yet sees elements of himself reflected in their behavior. The work requires entry into a space most investigators avoid. That tension gives the series much of its weight. Cases reach resolution, but the process leaves its mark. The cost of discernment is never fully removed.

Within the broader investigative structure, *Cracker* expands the concept of the team. The detective no longer carries the case alone, and even the Senior Investigating Officer relies on specialists from different disciplines. The profiler joins forensic experts, analysts, and investigators as part of a coordinated effort. Each contributes a distinct perspective. Fitz does not replace traditional policing. He alters its scope, adding a layer addressing motive and behavior alongside evidence and procedure.

The series extended into print through a small group of tie-in novels, some adapting episodes, others presenting original cases. These works maintain the focus on psychological analysis, reinforcing the central idea identifying the offender is only part of the task. Interpretation remains essential.

With *Cracker*, investigation turns inward in a new way. Structure and procedure remain necessary, but they are no longer sufficient. The work turns on interpretation, on the ability to read behavior and follow the internal logic driving it. A case is not complete until the person behind it is understood.

From this point, attention shifts again, away from interpretation and toward another form of specialization, one grounded not in psychology, but in science.

SILENT WITNESS—THE FORENSIC SCIENTIST

The modern investigation often begins not with a suspect, but with evidence. When *Silent Witness* premiered in 1996, it marked a decisive shift in British television detective drama. Attention moved away from the interview room and toward the laboratory, where the physical record of the crime could be examined with increasing precision and authority.

Dr. Sam Ryan, played by Amanda Burton, establishes this shift from the outset. As a forensic pathologist, her role does not involve pursuing suspects or conducting interrogations. She works with what remains, approaching the body as a source of information requiring careful, methodical reading. The process can be clinical and, at times, unsettling, yet it reveals something essential. The body records events in ways not easily altered. Injury, timing, and cause form a narrative independent of memory or testimony.

In this series, evidence does more than support an investigation. It directs it. Post-mortem findings, toxicology results, trace materials, and reconstruction of events determine the path forward. Earlier detective dramas used these elements as tools. Here, they become drivers. A case may begin in the laboratory, with conclusions shaping the direction of inquiry before a suspect is identified. The sequence reverses. Instead of building toward evidence, the investigation builds from it.

This shift alters how certainty is established. Forensic science introduces forms of proof grounded in physical reality rather than recollection. DNA analysis confirms identity. Blood pattern interpretation reveals movement and sequence. Digital evidence reconstructs timelines. Each element contributes to a framework capable of being tested and verified. The case no longer depends solely on what people say. It depends on what can be demonstrated.

The presence of forensic specialists reshapes the investigative structure. The Senior Investigating Officer continues to coordinate the case, but interpretation increasingly depends on those trained in specific disciplines. Pathologists, laboratory scientists, and technical experts contribute knowledge influencing direction and outcome. The investigation becomes collaborative at a deeper level, with each field providing a distinct layer of meaning.

As the series develops, particularly with Emilia Fox as Dr. Nikki Alexander, this collaborative model expands. Cases extend beyond isolated incidents into broader investigations involving organized crime, terrorism, and complex networks. Evidence links locations, individuals, and events across distance and time. The laboratory becomes a central node, where disparate strands are examined, compared, and connected into a coherent account.

Scientific work introduces its own pressures. Conclusions must be precise, defensible, and capable of withstanding scrutiny in court. A single misinterpretation can redirect an entire case. The process demands discipline, restraint, and attention to detail at every stage. Results are not accepted on instinct. They must be demonstrated, explained, and supported by method.

The series also highlights the limits of science. Evidence can establish sequence, cause, and connection, but it does not always explain intention. Motive still requires interpretation, often drawing the investigation back toward the human element. Science provides structure. Meaning emerges through integration with other forms of inquiry. The most effective investigations balance both.

Nigel McCrery extended the series into a small group of tie-in novels, which mirror this emphasis on forensic reconstruction. These stories treat evidence as narrative, showing how events can be rebuilt from physical traces. They reinforce the premise of solving a crime by depending on the ability to read what remains and to place it within a larger context.

Silent Witness presents investigation as a process grounded in physical proof. The detective remains responsible for directing the case, but meaning increasingly emerges from evidence and from those trained to interpret it. The work rests on coordination, precision, and the ability to translate scientific findings into a coherent account.

From this point, the focus shifts once more, away from immediate evidence and toward time itself, where cases remain unresolved and meaning must be recovered across years.

LINE OF DUTY—UNDER INVESTIGATION

By the time *Line of Duty* arrives, the detective story has already moved beyond the individual investigator and into the structure supporting the work. This series takes a further step by directing attention inward, placing the investigative process itself under scrutiny. The question no longer rests solely on who committed the crime. It extends to how the case was built, how decisions were justified, and whether the system can regulate itself.

At the center is AC-12, an anti-corruption unit tasked with examining the conduct of police officers suspected of misconduct. Their function differs from traditional detective work. Rather than pursuing external offenders, they review how cases are constructed, how authority is exercised, and whether procedure has been followed. The emphasis shifts from identifying events to evaluating the method used to establish them.

This development alters the balance of the narrative. Earlier portrayals followed detectives gathering evidence, interpreting behavior, and directing inquiries toward resolution. Here, the focus rests on the integrity of those actions. Files are reopened. Decisions are revisited. Events are reconstructed through documentation as well as testimony. A solved case no longer stands on outcome alone. It must be supported by a process capable of withstanding examination, and any weakness within that process becomes part of the story.

The interview room remains central, but its function changes. Questioning becomes structured, deliberate, and sustained. Officers are challenged on timelines, reports, and decisions, often over extended exchanges testing both patience and credibility. The objective is not simply to obtain admissions, but to expose inconsistency, identify contradiction, and establish patterns of conduct over time. These scenes carry a different tension. Movement is limited, but the stakes remain constant. A single answer can redirect the inquiry.

Precision defines these interviews. Every statement is cross-referenced. Every omission is noted. The process resembles interrogation as much as investigation, with pressure applied through persistence rather than force. Authority offers no protection. Rank may begin the exchange, but it does not determine its outcome. Consistency and evidence carry greater weight than position.

The series also reflects the layered complexity of modern policing. Authority operates across multiple levels, shaped by hierarchy, internal culture, and external pressure. Career advancement, reputation, and institutional priorities intersect with investigative decisions. The recurring reference to "bent coppers" suggests misconduct may not be confined to isolated individuals, but may extend into the structure itself. Suspicion moves upward as well as downward, creating an environment where trust remains provisional.

This dynamic introduces a further complication. The system investigates itself while simultaneously protecting itself. Decisions made in one department influence outcomes in another. Information is shared selectively. Loyalty competes with accountability. The inquiry becomes a negotiation between exposing misconduct and maintaining institutional stability. That tension shapes every case.

Within this framework, evidence extends beyond physical traces. Documentation, communications, surveillance footage, financial records, and procedural logs become central. The way a case is handled—what is recorded, what is omitted, how decisions are justified—forms part of the evidentiary record. Paperwork, often treated as background in earlier series, moves to the foreground and carries decisive weight.

Observation also evolves. Interviews are recorded. Actions are logged. Decisions are subject to review not only by supervisors, but by independent bodies and, indirectly, by the public. The detective operates within a system monitoring itself, creating layers of accountability. Each decision carries the potential to become evidence in a future inquiry.

Within this environment, the position of the detective changes again. No longer operating apart from the system, the investigator becomes subject to it. Conduct is examined alongside evidence. Judgment must account not only for immediate consequence, but for future scrutiny. The work requires an awareness that every action may later be revisited, reinterpreted, and challenged.

Resolution takes on a different meaning. A case may reach conclusion, but the method used to reach it remains open to review. Success becomes conditional. It depends not only on identifying the correct outcome, but on demonstrating that each step meets required standards. Process and result become inseparable.

Line of Duty presents policing as a profession in which integrity is not assumed, but tested. The investigation must establish both what occurred and how that conclusion was reached, showing that the work can withstand examination from within as well as from outside. The detective story becomes an inquiry into professional responsibility, where the central question extends beyond the crime to the system itself.

From here, attention shifts outward again, away from institutional scrutiny and toward the effect of crime on the community surrounding it.

BROADCHURCH—COMMUNITY

When a crime occurs in a small community, the impact extends beyond the immediate victim. It moves outward, affecting families, neighbors, and the social fabric holding the place together. *Broadchurch* centers on that expansion, treating the investigation not only as a search for an offender, but as an event reshaping an entire town.

Set in a coastal community where people know one another by name, the series begins with the death of a young boy. The case would carry weight in any setting, but familiarity intensifies its effect. The victim is known. His family is known. Those who may hold information are not distant witnesses, but members of the same social network, connected through work, school, and daily routine. The investigation unfolds within this web, where each question carries personal consequence.

Detective Inspector Alec Hardy, played by David Tennant, arrives as an outsider, assigned to lead a case in a town not his own. Detective Sergeant Ellie Miller, played by Olivia Colman, belongs to the community, familiar with its people and rhythms. Their partnership reflects two necessary perspectives. Hardy brings distance, focus, and resistance to local influence. Miller brings knowledge, trust, and an inherent grasp of how relationships operate. The investigation depends on both, even as those differences create tension.

The structure follows recognizable patterns, interviews, timelines, forensic results, and the gradual narrowing of possibilities. In *Broadchurch*, each step is embedded within the life of the community. Each interview becomes a moment of disruption. Each development alters relationships. Suspicion does not arrive openly. It moves quietly, reshaping how people see one another.

Grief becomes a constant presence. It extends beyond the immediate family, though the victim's parents remain central. It influences behavior, communication, and perception across the town. People hesitate. They withhold. They observe more closely. Memory becomes uncertain, shaped as much by emotion as by fact. The investigation proceeds through this atmosphere, where testimony carries both information and feeling.

Pacing reflects this reality. Scenes hold. Conversations pause. Silence acquires weight. Comprehension develops slowly, and the consequences of the crime continue to unfold long after initial discovery. The case advances, but the community moves with it, reacting, adjusting, and absorbing each development.

Media attention introduces further pressure. Journalists, particularly Karen White, played by Vicky McClure, alter the environment in which the investigation takes place. Information no longer remains contained. It is reported, interpreted, and broadcast. Rumor expands. Private grief becomes public. The detectives must manage not only the case, but the narrative surrounding it, aware that each disclosure can influence both perception and direction.

This pressure reshapes decision-making. Timing becomes critical. What is released, and when, carries consequence. A premature statement risks damaging the case. Withholding information invites speculation. The investigation unfolds within a space where information serves as both tool and liability, and control remains incomplete.

The series deepens its impact by extending beyond identification of the offender. The second season shifts into the courtroom, revisiting events already understood and placing them under renewed examination. Testimony is challenged. Evidence is reinterpreted. Decisions made during the investigation are scrutinized. The narrative turns back on itself, exposing gaps, assumptions, and pressures not fully visible earlier.

This transition introduces a different form of tension. The courtroom becomes another site of inquiry, where competing accounts are constructed and dismantled in public. The focus moves from discovery to validation. What matters is not only what is known, but what can be demonstrated and sustained under challenge. The detectives no longer direct the process. They observe it, confronting the possibility that earlier conclusions may not hold.

Trust within the community becomes more uncertain. Familiarity, once a source of stability, continues to complicate the search for truth. Every connection carries weight. Every revelation alters more than the case itself.

The strain on investigators becomes more pronounced. Miller's position grows increasingly difficult. Her connections, once an advantage, become a source of conflict. Hardy remains focused, but carries the weight of prior failure and the recognition that resolution does not end the work. The investigation continues, shaped by new interpretations as much as by new evidence.

Resolution does not restore the community to its previous state. The truth clarifies events, but also reveals how deeply relationships have shifted. The identification of the offender answers the central question, yet the consequences remain. The town continues with that knowledge, incorporating it into its sense of itself.

Within modern detective drama, *Broadchurch* emphasizes the environment in which crime occurs. Procedure and evidence remain essential, yet the investigation cannot be separated from those affected by it. The case is not an isolated problem. It is an event altering the place in which it unfolds.

The work extends beyond resolution. It requires awareness of consequence, and a perception of the outcome persisting long after the investigation closes.

From here, the focus narrows again, moving from the impact on a community to the experience of the individual officer who carries that weight over time.

HAPPY VALLEY—THE COST OF THE JOB

Policing, at its most immediate level, is lived day by day, case by case, often without clear separation between one incident and the next. *Happy Valley* returns the detective to that ground, focusing not on large systems or singular events, but on accumulation, the weight of repeated experience and the way it settles into the life of the officer carrying it.

Set in West Yorkshire, the series follows Sergeant Catherine Cawood, played by Sarah Lancashire, a uniformed officer positioned at the point of first contact with the public. Her responsibilities are broad. Domestic violence, addiction, theft, missing persons, and unpredictable incidents arising from daily life all fall within her remit. The range matters. It creates continuity. Each situation connects to others, forming a pattern rather than a series of isolated events.

Cawood's authority comes from experience rather than rank. She knows the people in her area, understands the rhythms of the community, and recognizes how minor disturbances can develop into something more serious. That awareness shapes her approach. She listens, observes, and intervenes early when possible, aware that prevention often matters as much as response. The work relies on judgment applied in real time, decisions made with incomplete information but informed by accumulated knowledge.

Happy Valley presents the relationship between professional duty and personal life as inseparable. Cawood's experience cannot be separated from her work. Her family history, particularly the death of her daughter and the presence of her grandson, connects directly to the crimes she encounters. The individual responsible remains within her orbit, creating sustained tension. The job does not end at the station door. It continues at home, in memory, and in the choices she makes about how far to pursue justice.

Violence appears not as isolated incidents, but as part of a wider social landscape. Crime emerges from circumstance, economic pressure, addiction, and patterns of behavior repeating across generations. Cases link through underlying conditions rather than through a single narrative thread. Resolution in one situation does not remove the factors producing the next. The environment remains constant, even as individual cases conclude.

Interviews reflect this immediacy. Cawood does not rely on elaborate strategy. She speaks directly, often confronting suspects with a mixture of authority and insight. Her strength lies in rapid assessment. She recognizes when someone is lying, when they are frightened, and when persuasion will fail. The approach is efficient, grounded in experience rather than theory.

Endurance becomes central. The job requires returning to the same streets, encountering the same individuals, and confronting the same problems over time. There is no sense of a reset. Each interaction adds to a growing accumulation of experience, shaping future responses. The detective carries this forward, whether acknowledged or not. Fatigue does not come from a single case. It develops gradually, built from repetition.

The series allows emotion to exist without dominating the work. Cawood is capable, controlled, and effective, yet affected by what she sees. Anger, grief, and frustration remain present, but they are managed. Strength lies not in detachment, but in the ability to continue despite the weight of experience. The balance between control and feeling defines her approach.

The long-term relationship between investigator and offender reinforces this pattern. Tommy Lee Royce, played by James Norton, represents a persistent presence rather than a single case. His influence extends across the series, linking past actions to present consequences. The conflict develops over time, shaped by memory and by the recognition that certain individuals do not disappear once a case concludes.

This continuity alters the meaning of resolution. Arrest and conviction do not end the story. The impact remains, influencing later decisions and shaping how new situations are approached. The work becomes cumulative. Each case contributes to a broader appreciation of how crime operates within the community and how it must be addressed.

Within the structure of modern detective drama, *Happy Valley* returns attention to the individual operating within the system. Procedure and oversight remain in place, yet the focus rests on how those elements are experienced at ground level, where decisions are immediate and consequences unfold quickly.

The profession here is shaped not by singular achievement, but by persistence. There is no final case resolving everything. There is only the next call, the next situation, and the continued responsibility to respond.

The cost of the work is not measured in a single moment. It accumulates over time, carried forward in memory, in judgment, and in the decisions shaping both the job and the life surrounding it.

From here, attention swings again, moving away from accumulation in the present and toward cases where time itself becomes the central obstacle to discernment.

UNFORGOTTEN—TIME AND THE BURIED PAST

Time does not erase crime. It alters its shape, disperses its evidence, and settles it into memory, but it does not remove it. *Unforgotten* builds its investigations around that principle, returning to cases long buried and examining how the passage of years changes both what is known and what can still be discovered.

Each investigation begins with a fragment. A body uncovered during construction. Remains discovered in an unexpected place. The initial discovery is often accidental, but what follows is deliberate. Detective Chief Inspector Cassie Stuart, played by Nicola Walker, and Detective Sergeant Sunil *Sunny* Khan, played by Sanjeev Bhaskar, lead inquiries moving backward as much as forward, reconstructing events occurring years, sometimes decades, earlier.

The structure of these investigations differs from contemporary cases. Evidence is incomplete. Records are missing or degraded. Witnesses have aged, relocated, or died. Memory becomes central, yet it remains unstable, shifting, fading, and reshaping itself over time. The detectives must navigate this uncertainty, distinguishing between recollection, omission, and concealment.

The pace reflects this condition. Progress develops gradually, with each piece of information requiring verification against a past no longer directly accessible. Interviews serve more than factual recovery. They reveal how events have been carried forward. A witness may recall an incident without sequence. A suspect may remember a detail without context. The investigation becomes reconstruction, assembling a coherent account from fragments that no longer align.

The series places particular emphasis on the lives built in the intervening years. Each suspect has established a present, careers formed, families created, identities reshaped. The earlier event remains beneath that surface, often unacknowledged yet never absent. When the investigation begins, it re-emerges, disrupting what has been constructed. The question extends beyond what happened to how that event continues to influence the present.

This approach expands the scope of consequence. Crime does not remain fixed at the moment of occurrence. It extends across years, affecting decisions, relationships, and self-perception. Guilt persists. Fear lingers. Silence becomes habit. The investigation exposes these continuities, revealing how a single act can shape multiple lives long after it occurred.

Cassie Stuart's method reflects this awareness. She proceeds with care, recognizing that those she questions have lived with these events for extended periods. Her approach allows space for recollection and acknowledgment. Sunny Khan provides balance, steady, methodical, and attentive to detail. Their partnership depends on consistency rather than urgency, returning to the same questions until the structure of the past begins to emerge.

The process depends on accumulation. No single discovery resolves the case. A document confirms a timeline. A statement introduces connection. A photograph reveals relationship. Each element contributes to a larger picture that only becomes visible through persistence. The work replaces immediacy with patience.

Time also alters responsibility. Those under investigation are not the same individuals they were at the moment of the crime. They have changed, adapted, and, in some cases, attempted to move beyond what occurred. The investigation must address both versions, the person who acted and the person who exists now. That distinction complicates judgment without removing it.

Reconstruction has limits. Evidence can establish sequence and connection, but intention may remain partially obscured. Memory can clarify, but it can also distort. The detectives work within those constraints, aware that certainty is often incomplete. The goal is not perfection, but clarity sufficient to bring the past into the present.

Resolution carries a different weight. Identification of those responsible does not restore what was lost, and it does not erase the years that have passed. It provides answers, but those answers arrive after long periods of uncertainty. Families receive acknowledgment. Those responsible confront actions deferred but not eliminated.

Within modern detective drama, *Unforgotten* places time at the center of the investigative process. Procedure remains essential. Evidence remains necessary. Both are shaped by delay. The work is shaped by the ability to move between past and present, recognizing that earlier events continue to exist in altered form.

In this setting, the detective operates as both investigator and interpreter of time. The task is not only to determine what occurred, but to understand how it has persisted, how it has been carried, and how it can finally be brought into the open.

From here, the focus shifts again, away from time as distance and toward place as defining condition, where environment shapes both crime and the method used to investigate it.

VERA—THE REGIONAL DETECTIVE

Northumberland stretches outward in long distances of coastline, farmland, and open moor, a landscape where movement takes time and where small communities exist both connected and apart. In *Vera*, this setting shapes the investigation from the outset. Geography determines access, limits opportunity, and influences how people live and interact. The case develops within these boundaries, defined as much by terrain and distance as by evidence.

Detective Chief Inspector Vera Stanhope, played by Brenda Blethyn, moves through this landscape with an approach that appears informal but is carefully controlled. She shows little concern for presentation or convention. Authority is expressed through presence rather than display. She observes, listens, and waits, allowing others to fill silence. Her strength lies in patience, persistence, and an ability to draw information through conversation rather than confrontation. Questions are often indirect, encouraging response and allowing inconsistencies to surface gradually.

The structure of each investigation reflects this method. Progress rarely follows a straight line. Information is gathered through repetition, returning to the same locations and the same individuals until patterns begin to emerge. What appears casual is deliberate. Vera allows space for people to speak, aware that omission can be as revealing as disclosure. A hesitation, a shift in tone, a detail introduced at the wrong moment, each becomes part of the evidentiary field.

This approach depends on time. The investigation circles rather than advances directly, revisiting earlier assumptions and testing them against new information. Small details gain weight when placed alongside others. Vera does not pursue immediate resolution. She allows the structure of the case to take shape, confident that persistence will produce clarity.

Community remains central. Crimes rarely emerge in isolation. They develop from relationships shaped by proximity, history, and familiarity. Individuals know one another's routines and associations. Knowledge can obscure as much as it reveals, creating assumptions requiring examination rather than acceptance. Loyalty, resentment, and obligation influence behavior, often quietly. Reading the case requires recognizing how relationships function within a particular place.

Continuity continues. Communities retain memory. Events are not erased so much as absorbed. Past conflicts, alliances, and grievances continue to influence present actions. Vera draws on this awareness, recognizing motive often lies in what has been carried forward. The investigation becomes a process of uncovering layers, bringing into view what has settled out of sight.

The investigative team provides structure, but direction remains closely tied to Vera's interpretation. Officers gather information, follow leads, and conduct interviews, yet meaning depends on how those elements are assembled. She listens to her team, but does not relinquish judgment. Authority is exercised through experience, guiding the work without overt assertion. Decisions emerge from awareness rather than hierarchy.

The landscape reinforces this method. Travel between locations takes time. Weather affects movement and access. Isolation can conceal activity, but also restricts options. A remote farmhouse, a stretch of coastline, or a rarely used road becomes part of the logic of the crime. Each element of the setting contributes to how events unfold and how they can be understood. The investigation adapts to these conditions, proceeding at a pace set by environment as much as by evidence.

Geography also shapes opportunity. It determines what can be done, when it can be done, and who might be present. The detective must consider not only motive, but access under specific conditions. Distance narrows possibilities while complicating them, requiring attention to detail and sequence.

The series draws from the novels of Ann Cleeves, beginning with *The Crow Trap* (1999) and continuing through a sequence rooted in Northumberland. Cleeves established a detective whose effectiveness depends on attention to place as well as to people. The adaptation retains this foundation, translating descriptive detail into visual form. The emphasis remains consistent. Behavior cannot be separated from context.

Cases often involve long-standing tensions, concealed histories, and relationships extending beyond immediate circumstances. Resolution depends on uncovering these connections. The investigation moves beyond surface detail toward comprehension shaped by environment, memory, and experience.

Vera presents detection as a process grounded in place, where geography, community, and personal history intersect. The work proceeds through observation, patience, and careful assembly of detail, drawing together multiple strands into an account reflecting both the crime and the conditions in which it occurred.

From here, the focus shifts further outward, toward a setting where isolation intensifies these conditions and where environment becomes even more decisive in shaping both crime and its investigation.

SHETLAND—ISOLATION AND ENVIRONMENT

The Shetland Islands sit on the northern edge of Britain, defined by sea, weather, and distance. Travel depends on ferries and flights, and conditions can delay or prevent movement altogether. In *Shetland*, these realities shape the investigation from the outset, setting limits on access, narrowing opportunity, and influencing how events unfold. Geography establishes the boundaries of the case before the first line of inquiry is pursued, and those limits remain present throughout.

Detective Inspector Jimmy Perez, played by Douglas Henshall, works within a community where familiarity and separation co-exist. The population is small enough for individuals to be known, yet the landscape allows distance between them. Lives spread across islands, farms, and small settlements, creating gaps in visibility affecting both crime and detection. Information is not always immediate, and absence can be as telling as presence.

Perez approaches the work with restraint and patience. He listens carefully, allowing conversations to unfold without pressure. His method relies on presence rather than confrontation, encouraging individuals to speak in their own time. In an environment where relationships are long-standing and trust is difficult to regain once lost, this approach becomes essential.

Progress often comes from returning to the same people and the same places, building a clearer picture through repetition and attention.

This patience is not passive. Perez observes closely, measuring responses, noting shifts in behavior, and allowing silence to carry weight. He recognizes that in a community where people are accustomed to one another, small changes carry significance. A hesitation, an avoided question, or a conversation cut short can reveal more than a direct denial. Noticing these details and placing them within a broader hierarchy of how individuals relate to one another is imperative.

The structure of the investigation reflects the constraints of the setting. Resources are limited, and specialist support is not always immediately available. The team works with what is at hand, adapting methods to suit conditions. Coordination remains important, but it operates within narrower limits than in larger urban investigations. Each decision carries weight, with fewer opportunities to redirect or recover from error. A missed detail may not be quickly corrected. A delay may alter the course of the case.

Isolation also affects time. Movement cannot be assumed. Travel must be planned, and delays are common. The investigation advances in stages shaped by access rather than urgency alone. This creates a different rhythm, one requiring adjustment rather than acceleration. The detective works within these limits, recognizing control is partial and progress depends on conditions beyond the immediate case. The landscape influences behavior in direct ways. Harsh weather, open water, and long distances shape how people move, where they go, and what they are able to do. Movement can be tracked through necessity rather than surveillance. Travel requires planning, and absence becomes noticeable. Opportunity is defined by geography, and motive often connects to the pressures of living in a place where isolation is constant.

A psychological dimension underlies isolation. Distance from larger centers creates a sense of containment. Lives unfold in close proximity to the same people, places, and histories. Conflicts do not easily dissipate. Relationships persist over time, carrying both loyalty and tension. The investigation must account for this continuity, recognizing behavior is shaped by conditions extending beyond the immediate moment.

The emotional impact of crime is intensified by proximity. In a setting where anonymity is limited, events resonate across the community. Individuals connect through family, work, and shared history. A single incident affects multiple lives, and those effects continue long after the initial event. The investigation must account for these connections, recognizing responses to the crime may shape what is revealed and what remains concealed.

The series is based on the novels of Ann Cleeves, whose *Shetland* books established both the character of Perez and the importance of the island setting. Cleeves also created *Vera*, yet the two adaptations diverge in emphasis. Where *Vera* explores breadth and accumulated history across a wider region, *Shetland* focuses on containment, using geography to compress relationships and intensify scrutiny. Early seasons draw directly from the novels, while later episodes extend beyond them, maintaining the same emphasis on environment and character.

A shift occurs when Perez leaves the series. Detective Inspector Ruth Calder, played by Ashley Jensen, returns to Shetland after time spent on the mainland. Her experience introduces a different perspective. She has absorbed the setting, but no longer belongs to it in the same way. That distance allows her to question assumptions others accept, while familiarity provides context for interpreting behavior. She sees both what fits and what does not, bridging two viewpoints without fully settling into either.

This change alters the dynamic of the investigation. Where Perez moved within the community as part of it, Calder operates with partial separation. That difference influences how information is received and evaluated. The work remains grounded in place, but interpretation becomes more explicit, examined rather than assumed.

The investigative process continues to depend on careful observation and measured judgment. Evidence must be considered alongside the conditions in which it appears. Actions are evaluated in relation to geography, access, and opportunity, and conclusions emerge through gradual assembly of detail rather than rapid deduction. The pace remains steady, shaped by setting as much as by the case itself.

Shetland presents detection shaped directly by isolation. The setting defines the limits of the investigation, influences behavior, and determines how the work proceeds. Reading the crime requires reading place, and the investigation advances through patience, awareness, and attention to the conditions governing life on the islands.

THE FALL—THE HUNTER

In some investigations, the relationship between detective and offender becomes the central focus. *The Fall* builds its structure around this connection, presenting a case in which both identities are established early, shifting attention toward the space between them and the consequences developing over time.

Set in Belfast, the narrative follows Detective Superintendent Stella Gibson, played by Gillian Anderson, as she leads the search for a serial offender, Paul Spector, portrayed by Jamie Dornan. From the outset, access is granted to both perspectives. The case does not unfold as a question of identity, but as a sustained examination of behavior, intention, and control. The movement between hunter and hunted clarifies rather than conceals, allowing the dynamics of pursuit to define the structure.

Gibson approaches the case with precision and distance. Authority is direct, method controlled. She evaluates evidence, directs resources, and maintains focus on patterns shaping the offender's actions. Language remains exact. Decisions are deliberate. Distraction is resisted, with progress dependent on consistency and clarity. In contrast, Spector operates within a private logic shaped by compulsion and self-justification. He maintains a surface life concealing his actions, moving between routine and calculated violence. Tension emerges from the coexistence of these two worlds, one governed by structure, the other by impulse.

The Fall examines the consequences of violence with unusual depth. Victims are not reduced to narrative function. Their absence shapes the lives of those around them, and the series allows space for that impact to register. Families respond with grief, confusion, and anger. Colleagues attempt to reconstruct what has been lost. The case advances within this environment, where each development carries emotional as well as procedural weight.

The effect on investigators is equally present. Gibson maintains professional distance, yet remains fully aware of the stakes. Repetition of the crimes, clarity of intent, and knowledge of potential escalation create sustained pressure. Control is required, but awareness cannot be removed. The work continues within that tension.

The relationship between Gibson and Spector develops through indirect contact before becoming explicit. Each studies the other. Gibson reconstructs behavior through pattern and evidence. Spector monitors the progress of the inquiry, adjusting his actions as necessary. This produces a form of interaction preceding physical confrontation, where established belief becomes engagement. Distance narrows first at an intellectual level, long before proximity becomes possible.

Beyond the individual case, the series engages with a broader social framework. Violence is not presented as isolated or inexplicable. It is situated within issues of gender, power, and perception. The selection of victims, the nature of the crimes, and the offender's internal justification point toward a pattern of control. Gibson articulates this clearly, placing the case within a wider context concerning how women are perceived and targeted.

Her perspective extends the scope of the investigation beyond immediate circumstances.

This dimension shapes interpretation. The crimes are not treated as singular acts, but as expressions of a pattern reflecting underlying attitudes. The work includes recognizing and articulating that pattern, even when doing so moves beyond conventional procedural boundaries. The case becomes both specific and representative, tied to individual responsibility and broader context.

Observation becomes central to both sides. Investigator and offender operate within overlapping systems of surveillance. Gibson relies on records, coordination, and structured inquiry. Spector relies on anonymity, routine, and the ability to move without notice. Each watches the other, directly or indirectly. The act of seeing carries significance, defining who holds knowledge and who remains exposed.

When the investigation reaches confrontation, emphasis remains on consequence rather than spectacle. The capture of the offender does not produce a simple resolution. Questions persist regarding responsibility, impact, and the limits of certainty. The narrative resists a clean division between conclusion and aftermath, allowing consequences to extend beyond the moment of arrest.

Within modern detective drama, *The Fall* presents investigation as a sustained encounter between opposing forms of control. Procedure remains essential, yet is accompanied by interpretation and awareness of the broader framework in which the crimes occur.

The detective must do more than identify and apprehend. The work requires a clear knowledge of what the crime represents, how it affects those involved, and how it fits within a larger pattern. Resolution closes the case, but the implications remain.

GRACE—THE BURDEN OF THE PAST

Brighton is defined by movement and contrast, a coastal city where visitors arrive and depart in steady flow, and where anonymity exists alongside familiarity. In *Grace*, this environment frames an approach to detection combining contemporary procedure with a persistent connection to unresolved events.

Detective Superintendent Roy Grace, played by John Simm, leads major inquiries within a structured system built on coordination and control. Teams are assigned. Evidence is processed through established channels. Lines of inquiry develop across multiple fronts, supported by forensic analysis, digital tracking, surveillance, and interview work. The structure reflects modern policing at full scale, where progress depends on managing information as much as discovering it.

Within this framework, Grace functions as both director and interpreter. Decisions determine priority, allocate resources, and shape the direction of the inquiry. The role requires constant assessment, weighing competing lines of evidence and adjusting strategy as new information emerges. The work proceeds through organization, yet remains dependent on judgment applied under pressure.

Alongside this structure runs a personal history that alters perspective. The unexplained disappearance of Grace's wife remains unresolved, placing him in the position of directing inquiries while living with a case lacking conclusion. This absence introduces a different dimension to his approach. He knows not only how cases are built, but how they persist when resolution does not arrive. The distinction between professional responsibility and personal experience becomes less defined.

This dual awareness influences how he engages with ongoing inquiries. Cases involving missing persons or incomplete evidence carry particular weight. Attention extends beyond immediate facts to what may have been overlooked, misinterpreted, or left unexamined. The investigation becomes both forward-moving and reflective, shaped by procedure and by recognition of uncertainty.

The series allows movement between present-day cases and earlier events. Current inquiries unfold through established method, while elements of the past continue to inform decisions. This interplay creates a layered structure, where each development is considered not only in isolation, but in relation to what preceded it. Patterns emerge across time, linking separate moments into a broader sensibility.

Cold case work introduces additional complexity. Interest in older investigations competes with demands of active cases, where urgency directs resources elsewhere. Grace's persistence reflects a different view. Time does not diminish significance. It alters conditions under which evidence must be evaluated. Records may be incomplete. Witnesses may be difficult to locate. Memory may be unreliable. Even so, the need for clarity remains.

This perspective shapes interaction with victims and families. Communication carries awareness of what it means to live without resolution. The work involves establishing fact while acknowledging absence, addressing both what can be proven and what continues to be unknown. Balance becomes essential, maintaining objectivity while recognizing the human impact of uncertainty.

The investigative process remains grounded in coordination. Specialists contribute expertise, each element forming part of a larger structure. Forensic findings establish sequence. Digital records trace movement. Interviews provide context. No single component resolves the case. Progress depends on integration, bringing together multiple strands into a coherent account.

This integration extends to the way past and present are treated. Earlier actions, overlooked details, and connections across time contribute to development of the inquiry. Reconstruction becomes necessary, linking fragments into a unified narrative. The detective must consider not only what occurred, but how it will evolve as new information is introduced.

Peter James's novels establish this dual framework, combining detailed procedural work with an ongoing personal narrative. The adaptation retains that balance, presenting cases grounded in modern practice while maintaining continuity across episodes. The character is shaped as much by what remains unresolved as by what is successfully concluded.

The result is a form of detection operating at the intersection of method and memory. Structured procedure provides the means to advance the inquiry, while experience introduces awareness of what may remain incomplete. Each case reflects both the capacity of the system to resolve and its limits when confronted with uncertainty.

Grace brings together elements developed throughout the modern era. Organized investigation, specialized expertise, psychological awareness, and the persistence of unresolved events converge within a single framework. The detective functions not only as a coordinator of information, but as a figure carrying forward the concept some questions extend beyond immediate resolution.

From here, the focus moves toward the next stage of development, where the modern system is inherited and reshaped by those entering the profession under entirely different expectations.

INSPECTOR ELLIS—MODERN DETECTIVE

By this stage of modern British detective drama, the separate elements of investigation—procedure, forensic science, behavioral analysis, oversight, public scrutiny, and environment—no longer operate in isolation. *Inspector Ellis* presents a form of policing in which these components function together, each contributing to a structure dependent on coordination rather than specialization alone.

The detective at the center works within a fully developed framework. Cases are structured from the outset. Teams carry defined responsibilities. Information is gathered across multiple channels and assessed as part of a larger whole. Forensic results, digital records, witness accounts, and surveillance material are not treated as independent strands. Their meaning emerges through connection, each piece gaining weight when considered alongside others.

This approach alters the nature of the work. Progress no longer depends on a single breakthrough or a dominant line of inquiry. It develops through the steady alignment of multiple forms of information. A timeline established through digital data must correspond with physical evidence. A statement must hold when measured against behavior and circumstance. The investigation advances through correlation, not sequence.

Leadership adapts to this environment. The role requires direction without overreach, maintaining clarity while allowing the process to evolve. Resources must be assigned with purpose. Priorities must be set and revised as conditions change. Decisions are made continuously, often without complete information, and must remain flexible enough to accommodate new developments. Authority is expressed through organization and judgment, ensuring each part of the inquiry contributes to a coherent outcome.

The pace reflects this complexity. Movement occurs across several fronts at once. One team may pursue witnesses while another examines forensic results and a third analyzes digital evidence. These efforts converge gradually, requiring careful management to prevent fragmentation. The detective must track progress across all areas, recognizing how each development influences the others.

Documentation becomes central. Every action must be recorded with precision. Procedures must be followed and, when necessary, justified. The process itself forms part of the evidentiary record. Decisions are subject to review, both within the department and beyond it. This introduces a further layer of responsibility. The investigation must not only reach the correct conclusion, but demonstrate how that conclusion was achieved.

Oversight operates as a constant presence. Internal review examines conduct. External scrutiny shapes perception. The detective works within a framework where accountability is immediate and ongoing. Each decision carries the potential for later examination. Awareness of this reality influences how the work is conducted, encouraging consistency, clarity, and discipline at every stage.

However, the human dimension remains essential. Victims, families, and communities continue to shape the direction of the inquiry. Their responses influence priorities and affect how information is received. The detective must balance structural demands with an insight into the impact on individuals, recognizing effective investigation depends on both.

The series incorporates elements earlier dramas explored individually, bringing them into a single operating model. Behavioral insight informs how suspects are approached and understood. Forensic analysis provides measurable evidence capable of verification. Coordination across teams ensures information is shared and evaluated efficiently. Oversight introduces accountability. Public attention influences how the case is managed and how its progress is perceived.

Integration requires a different form of expertise. The detective must understand each component while recognizing how they interact. Evidence gains meaning through context. Behavior must be evaluated alongside circumstance. Decisions must account for immediate needs as well as longer-term implications. The work becomes one of synthesis, bringing together diverse forms of knowledge into a unified interpretation.

Experience remains a guiding factor. Patterns recognized from earlier cases inform present decisions, shaping how new information is assessed. Knowledge accumulates over time, refining judgment and improving the ability to recognize connection. Even within a highly structured system, individual insight retains value, not as a substitute for process, but as a complement to it.

The investigation unfolds through continuous adjustment. Information is tested, connections are identified, and priorities shift as new details emerge. No single path defines the inquiry. Multiple lines develop and converge, requiring ongoing coordination to maintain direction. Managing this complexity becomes central to the role.

Inspector Ellis presents a view of policing in which effectiveness depends on integration. The detective operates as both participant and organizer, working within the system while directing its movement. Success depends not on any single method, but on the ability to align multiple elements into a coherent and defensible account.

From here, the modern structure gives way to something different, where the system is no longer the defining force, and the detective once again stands apart from it.

CASE SUMMARY

In the modern era, the detective story shifts from individual pursuit to coordinated effort. The central figure remains, but no longer carries the case alone. The work expands outward into teams, systems, and processes shaping how inquiries develop and conclude.

Earlier approaches relied on instinct, experience, and personal interpretation. Those qualities remain, but now operate within a broader framework. Coordination, specialization, and accountability define progress. The detective directs, but does not act in isolation.

Each series contributes to this structure. *Tennison* shows the emergence of the modern investigator. *Prime Suspect* defines leadership within major inquiries. *Cracker* expands the field through psychological interpretation. *Silent Witness* places physical evidence at the center of the case. *Line of Duty* turns attention toward accountability within the institution.

Other series extend the scope further. *Broadchurch* places inquiry under public scrutiny. *Happy Valley* grounds the work in frontline reality. *Unforgotten* shows how time reshapes perception. *Vera* and *Shetland* demonstrate how place defines both crime and method. *The Fall* examines the relationship between investigator and offender. *Grace* integrates unresolved past with present inquiry. *Inspector Ellis* brings these elements together, presenting investigation as a fully integrated system.

These portrayals define detection as a coordinated process built on precision and cooperation. Evidence is tested. Decisions are examined. Method becomes as important as outcome. Success depends not only on resolving the case, but on showing how each conclusion was reached and sustained under scrutiny.

The detective remains essential, but the role has changed. No longer defined by a single skill or perspective, the modern investigator operates within a network of expertise, drawing on multiple forms of knowledge to reach a conclusion. Reading people remains central, but it is now achieved through the integration of insight, evidence, and coordinated effort reflecting the complexity of contemporary policing.

Beyond this structure lies a different tradition, where the detective stands apart from the system and the work follows a different logic.

PART FIVE

THE AMATEURS & ODDBALLS

These detectives solve crimes not through rank or procedure, but through intellect, observation, and the force of personality.

INTRODUCTION—THE INDIVIDUAL MIND

A distinct group operates outside formal systems entirely, working without rank, without official authority, and often without permission. They are not assigned cases. They find them, are drawn into them, or refuse to let them go. British television has long made space for these figures, outsiders, independents, and unconventional thinkers approaching crime from a different direction. Their presence suggests investigation is not confined to institutions, and solutions can emerge from places the system does not reach.

These detectives are not defined by procedure. Many are amateurs, though the label does not fully capture their role. They operate independently. They do not rely on chain of command, formal process, or organizational expectation. Instead, they depend on intellect, observation, experience, or instinct. Where the working detective builds a case through method, the outsider often resolves it through perception. Where the professional follows established steps, the independent mind moves in directions the system cannot permit.

This freedom allows a different form of inquiry. Questions can be asked without regard for protocol. Conversations unfold without the constraints of an official interview. Lines of inquiry are pursued without advance justification. The absence of structure creates opportunity, but removes support. There is no access to records without permission, no authority to compel answers, no guarantee conclusions will be accepted. Effectiveness depends entirely on the ability to recognize what matters and act on it.

British television returns to this figure repeatedly, not as a replacement for the professional, but as a counterpoint. The consulting detective, the observant amateur, the specialist with deep knowledge in a narrow field, the eccentric mind recognizing patterns others miss, each represents a different approach to the same problem. These figures move through environments resisting formal inquiry, drawing rooms, colleges, galleries, archives, and private conversations where information is guarded by custom rather than law. They navigate social spaces as carefully as others navigate crime scenes.

A long literary tradition supports these characters. Sherlock Holmes, Miss Marple, and Hercule Poirot established detection as an intellectual pursuit as much as a professional obligation. British television inherits and extends this tradition, widening the range of who can solve a crime and how it can be approached. In these stories, the detective is not always a representative of the law. Sometimes the detective is simply the person who understands the situation more clearly than anyone else.

As policing becomes more structured, more procedural, and more closely supervised, the appeal of the independent detective increases. These figures offer an alternative perspective, one emphasizing thought over process, insight over coordination. They remind us crime is not only a matter of evidence and procedure, but also of motive, behavior, and the ways people conceal or reveal themselves.

The variety within this group is considerable. Some are precise and controlled, applying disciplined reasoning to every detail. Others are distracted, eccentric, or socially out of step, arriving at conclusions through indirect paths. Some possess deep expertise in a particular field—art, literature, history, science—and use it to interpret what others cannot. Others rely on observation and instinct, recognizing patterns without fully articulating how. Their differences matter as much as their similarities, demonstrating there is no single model of independent detection.

What unites them is distance. They stand apart from structures defining the professional detective. That separation allows them to see what others miss, but places them in a position where conclusions must often be translated into action by someone else. Insight alone is not enough. It must intersect with authority before a case can be resolved.

This section considers those individuals operating in the area between awareness and action, between independence and necessity. They approach crime as a problem to be interpreted rather than a case to be processed, and success depends on how effectively they move between those positions.

They do not fit comfortably within the systems surrounding them. That discomfort gives them value. They look where others do not, ask what others will not, and recognize what others fail to see.

SHERLOCK—CONSULTING DETECTIVE

An outlier intellect can see a solution before a question is fully understood. A glance, a gesture, the condition of a sleeve, the ash on a cuff, and the pattern resolves. In the Granada television adaptation of *Sherlock Holmes*, this is not presented as trickery or convenience, but as disciplined observation carried to an extreme. The detective does not simply gather facts. He sees them differently.

Portrayed by Jeremy Brett, Holmes becomes more than a familiar literary figure. He is not a comfortable genius or an eccentric indulgence. He is precise, restless, and often difficult, a man whose mind moves faster than the world around him and grows impatient when others cannot keep pace. Brett's performance emphasizes the physicality of thought, sudden shifts of attention, intensity of focus, and abrupt transitions from stillness to movement. Thinking becomes visible, an active, almost exhausting process driving everything he does. The effect is to make deduction feel less like explanation and more like pursuit, a mind pressing forward before ordinary conversation has caught up.

Holmes stands apart within British detective storytelling through complete independence. He holds no rank, answers to no superior, and follows no formal procedure beyond the one he constructs for himself. The police consult him when their methods reach a limit. He does not replace the system. He supplements it, moving where it cannot and seeing what it overlooks. Where the working detective builds a case through accumulation, Holmes arrives at conclusions through pattern, inference, and disciplined elimination of the impossible. He is free to begin with what appears marginal, insignificant, or unlikely, because he does not need to justify his first instinct to anyone.

The Granada series ensured this approach remained grounded. Settings are detailed, pacing deliberate, and each case unfolds with careful attention to cause and effect. Holmes does not succeed because the narrative requires it. He succeeds because he notices what others ignore and draws conclusions others would hesitate to make. Each investigation becomes an exercise in perception, demonstrating how the smallest detail, properly understood, can carry the weight of proof. The method is unusual, but the logic is rigorous. Once Holmes explains what he has seen, the extraordinary often proves entirely practical.

At the center of this dynamic stands Dr. Watson, played by David Burke and later Edward Hardwicke. Watson is not merely an assistant. He is the necessary counterbalance, the observer who translates Holmes' reasoning into something the audience can follow. He asks the questions others would ask, notes what others would notice, and provides a steady presence against which Holmes' intensity can be measured. Without Watson, the process remains internal. With him, it becomes visible. Just as important, Watson supplies a moral and emotional steadiness Holmes himself does not always possess, keeping the detective connected to ordinary human consequence.

Holmes' relationship with official policing further defines his role. Figures such as Inspector Lestrade represent professional investigation, methodical, procedural, and constrained by evidence and expectation. Holmes operates alongside them, but never within their limits. He speculates freely, tests improbable theories, and pursues lines of inquiry unlikely to survive official scrutiny. In doing so, he reveals both the strengths and the limits of formal policing. The police can secure a scene, gather statements, and enforce the law. Holmes can recognize the hidden pattern before the larger machinery is ready to move.

The adaptation's fidelity to the stories of Arthur Conan Doyle reinforces this position. Episodes draw closely from the canon, preserving plot, tone, atmosphere, and structure. This fidelity makes clear Holmes' approach is not a modern interpretation imposed on a Victorian setting. It is fully formed, existing alongside the professionalization of policing rather than emerging from it. He is not an early version of the modern detective. He is a parallel tradition. This distinction matters, because it explains why Holmes continues to feel singular even after generations of detectives have followed him.

Holmes represents the purest expression of the individual detective. He is not shaped by institution, rank, or procedure. He is shaped by intellect. His effectiveness depends entirely on how he observes, how he reasons, and how far he is willing to follow a conclusion once it forms. There is no structure to support him and no system to contain him. There is only the problem and the mind brought to bear on it.

This independence explains his lasting influence. Nearly every detective who follows, whether professional or amateur, exists in relation to him. Some adopt elements of his approach. Others define themselves in opposition. Many attempt to balance intellect with procedure in ways he never needed to consider. Yet the central idea remains unchanged: a single individual, thinking clearly enough and looking closely enough, can understand what others cannot.

Through Holmes, the consulting detective stands apart from the working detective not because he is more capable, but because he is unconstrained. He answers only to the logic of the case and the conclusions it demands.

HERCULE POIROT—THE LITTLE GREY CELLS

Order governs everything in *Agatha Christie's Poirot*. Before the crime is explained, before the culprit is named, the world must first be set into proper relation. Facts are arranged. Motives are weighed. Contradictions are tested. Detection becomes less an act of pursuit than an act of placement, each detail set where it belongs until confusion gives way to design.

Portrayed by David Suchet, Hercule Poirot is defined by precision. Appearance, manners, and thought all reflect a desire for symmetry and control. Nothing is left to chance. Clothing is exact. Objects are properly placed. Conversations are guided with intention. This attention to order is not eccentricity for its own sake. It forms the basis of his method. Poirot believes a properly arranged world will disclose the truth.

Where Holmes observes, Poirot interprets. The clues carrying greatest weight are not always physical. They emerge in behavior, contradiction, and the way a person speaks or avoids speaking. He studies motive, vanity, fear, and deception, assembling not only what happened, but why. Crime becomes a problem of human nature, and its solution depends on knowing character as much as circumstance.

The series reinforces this through structure. Poirot does not rush toward conclusion. He gathers people, listens carefully, and allows inconsistency to surface. The familiar drawing room scene, with suspects assembled and the solution revealed, is not merely theatrical. It is the final movement of a process already completed in his mind. By the time Poirot explains the crime, discovery has ended. What remains is arrangement, the placing of each fact in proper relation to the others.

This reliance on arrangement gives the detective story a particular shape. The audience sees the same details, hears the same statements, and observes the same behavior, yet comprehension depends on how those elements are ordered. Poirot's gift lies not in access to hidden information, but in the ability to impose structure on what appears scattered. Truth is often already present, obscured by misdirection, vanity, or emotional confusion.

Set largely in the interwar period, the series creates a world of contained environments, country houses, trains, hotels, and carefully managed social spaces. These settings reinforce Poirot's method. Crime occurs within a defined structure, and the solution remains within the same boundary. Unlike the working detective, who navigates open systems and unpredictable conditions, Poirot operates within closed circles, where every suspect can be identified and every movement can, at least in theory, be accounted for.

Agatha Christie's literary foundation of the character is central to this design. Christie's view of the detective story as puzzle, governed by fairness and logic, finds its fullest expression in Poirot. The television adaptation preserves the architecture. Each case unfolds as an intellectual exercise, but one rooted in human weakness rather than abstraction. Jealousy, greed, pride, humiliation, and fear all appear beneath the polished surfaces of polite society. Poirot's task is to recognize how disorder enters a world committed to appearances.

Poirot represents the disciplined mind. He imposes order on chaos. He does not rely on force, rank, or institutional support. His effectiveness lies in the ability to see structure where others see confusion, to recognize patterns of behavior, and to understand the emotional logic driving the crime. He is not outside the system in quite the way Holmes is, nor inside it in the manner of the working detective. He occupies a space defined by method alone.

There is, however, a limit to this approach. Poirot's world depends on containment. His method works best when variables can be controlled, suspects gathered, and the problem reduced to a set of relationships. It is a form of detection thriving on clarity. When crime moves beyond defined spaces into larger, less stable environments, the method becomes harder to sustain.

Even so, Poirot's influence remains considerable. He establishes detection can be an act of arrangement as much as discovery, motive can matter as much as opportunity, and the solution may lie not in what has been hidden, but in what has been misunderstood.

Poirot shows the detective does not always need to move faster or look harder. Sometimes the essential task is to think more clearly, place each fact where it belongs, and allow the pattern to emerge.

MISS MARPLE—THE HUMAN EQUATION

Recognition comes first for Miss Marple. Before evidence is assembled or conclusions proposed, she identifies the kind of person who would commit the act. In the television adaptations, the solution does not begin at the scene, but in behavior. A glance, a hesitation, a familiar form of deception, each carries meaning. The crime is understood not as an isolated event, but as part of a pattern already known.

Portrayed across adaptations by Joan Hickson, Geraldine McEwan, and Julia McKenzie, Jane Marple appears an unlikely detective. She is elderly, unassuming, and rooted in village routine. Nothing suggests urgency or authority. This position provides advantage. She is overlooked, and because she is overlooked, she observes without interference. Attention settles elsewhere, leaving her free to study what others dismiss.

Her method depends on analogy. One case is never separate from another. A suspect in a country house recalls someone from the village. A particular lie resembles one told years earlier. A gesture, a tone of voice, a moment of hesitation, all connect to prior experience. Human behavior, in her view, is consistent. People repeat themselves. Motives recur. Weaknesses persist. By recognizing these patterns, she sees what others cannot. The present becomes legible through the past.

This approach shapes how she moves through a case. Rather than advancing step by step through evidence, she forms an early impression of character and tests it against what she sees and hears. Details confirm or contradict this impression. Conversations matter as much as objects. A misplaced emphasis, a story told too carefully, or a remark offered too quickly can reveal more than physical proof. The investigation develops through attention, not pursuit.

The settings support this way of working. Villages, small communities, and contained social environments dominate the series. These are places where familiarity suggests openness, yet concealment thrives beneath it. Miss Marple understands proximity does not prevent deception. It enables it. The closer people are, the more effectively they hide what they prefer not to reveal. Courtesy becomes camouflage. Routine becomes cover. She moves through these spaces with quiet authority, grounded in knowledge of how people behave when they believe themselves safe.

The character—again created by the great Agatha Christie—rests on careful observation of human inconsistency. Small details reveal larger truths. The adaptations preserve this emphasis, presenting each case as an examination of motive, relationship, and concealed intent. Crime is not treated as a puzzle alone, but as an expression of character shaped by circumstance and opportunity.

Her conclusions arrive without display. There is no need to command a room or construct a dramatic reveal. When she speaks, the explanation carries weight because it reflects insight rather than deduction alone. Others may resist or dismiss her at first, but the clarity of her reasoning leaves little room for doubt once it is fully expressed.

Her position also shapes how information is gathered. People speak freely in her presence. They underestimate her, confide in her, or reveal more than intended in casual conversation. She does not interrogate. She listens. Information accumulates indirectly, often without the speaker realizing its significance. What appears harmless becomes essential when placed alongside what she already knows.

Her strength lies in recognizing how ordinary behavior conceals extraordinary intent. Nothing appears unusual until it is viewed in the right context. A minor inconsistency becomes decisive. A familiar pattern reveals a hidden motive. She does not need access to every fact. She needs only enough to confirm what she already understands.

This approach has limits. It depends on proximity, on the ability to observe closely and relate behavior to known patterns. It functions best in connected environments where relationships carry history and meaning. In settings defined by anonymity, where individuals remain unknown to one another, the method loses most of its force. Without familiarity, comparison becomes harder to sustain.

Even so, Miss Marple's influence remains considerable. She demonstrates detection can rest on recognition rather than deduction, and the solution may lie not in evidence alone, but in the nature of the people involved. Her method shifts the essential investigative question from what happened to who would do such a thing, and why.

ART DETECTIVES—THE SPECIALIST EYE

Works of art can conceal as much as they reveal. Meaning lies in detail, in provenance, in the history carried beneath the surface. In *Art Detectives*, the question is not always what is missing, but what has been misunderstood. Paintings, artifacts, and cultural objects carry histories, and those histories become part of the investigation.

The series follows Detective Inspector Mick Palmer, played by Stephen Moyer, and Detective Constable Shazia Malik, played by Nina Singh, working within the Metropolitan Police's Heritage Crime Unit. Their cases involve murder, theft, and fraud connected to the art world, where value is rarely obvious and authenticity is often contested. A painting may be genuine or forged. An object may be priceless or negligible, details only a trained eye can read with confidence.

Knowledge drives the investigation. The detective does not simply collect facts, but interprets them through a specialized lens. Provenance, technique, materials, and historical context function as evidence. A brushstroke, a signature, or the aging of a surface may carry as much weight as physical proof. Meaning does not reside in the object alone. It emerges through knowledge of how and why it exists.

This changes the rhythm of the work. The investigation moves less through pursuit than through interpretation. Leads develop through research, consultation, and the gradual assembling of context. Archives are examined. Experts are consulted. Connections form between past and present. A stolen object may have passed through multiple hands across decades, each transfer adding another layer of meaning. The case unfolds across time as well as place.

Authenticity becomes a central question. Determining whether an object is genuine often determines motive, opportunity, and value. A forgery may be created for profit, deception, or prestige. A genuine work may be stolen for reasons extending beyond money, including reputation, control, or personal obsession. Establishing authenticity requires attention to detail beyond the reach of general investigation. Knowledge becomes the tool used to reveal intent.

Still the human element remains constant. The crimes are still driven by greed, ambition, deception, and opportunity. The art provides context, but behavior provides direction. Palmer brings experience and instinct, recognizing patterns of conduct and motive. Malik contributes a contemporary perspective, combining analytical thinking with familiarity with evolving investigative methods. Their partnership balances traditional detection with specialized knowledge, allowing each case to develop across both domains.

The environments further shape the investigation. Museums, galleries, private collections, and auction houses become active spaces, each governed by its own expectations and forms of discretion. Legitimacy can conceal illegality. Access depends on credibility. The detective must move within these spaces with an ability to read how they operate, speaking the language of the field while identifying where language is used to obscure the truth.

These settings introduce another layer of complexity. Objects often carry legal, historical, and cultural implications extending beyond ownership. Questions of restitution, provenance gaps, and contested heritage can influence how a case is approached. What appears to be theft may involve claims reaching back generations. Resolution requires attention not only to the immediate crime, but to the broader context surrounding the object.

The investigative process depends on aligning these elements. Physical evidence, expert interpretation, historical context, and human motive must be brought into relation. No single piece is sufficient on its own. Meaning emerges through combination, each part reinforcing or challenging the others. The detective becomes a coordinator of knowledge, ensuring each element contributes to a coherent grasp of the case.

This form of detection reflects a wider shift. As crime becomes more specialized, so does the response. Financial investigations require knowledge of systems and markets. Digital crime demands technical expertise. Cultural crime depends on familiarity with history, value, and context. The detective extends beyond observation and questioning into areas requiring sustained study and experience.

Art Detectives presents detectives defined not by rank or independence, but by depth of niche wisdom. Knowing what others cannot recognize is the key. A detail overlooked by most becomes decisive when placed within the correct framework. The key is not attention, but comprehension.

It shows solving a crime may depend not only on seeing clearly or reasoning effectively, but on knowing enough to understand what is seen. Without this knowledge, the evidence remains incomplete, even when fully visible.

THE CHINESE DETECTIVE—OUTSIDER

Distance sharpens perception. In *The Chinese Detective*, the advantage lies not in authority or force, but in the ability to see from more than one position at once. The detective understands the world he works in, yet recognizes where he does not fully belong, and uses this as an advantage to read what others miss.

Detective Sergeant John Ho, played by David Yip, operates within the Metropolitan Police while remaining distinct from it. He is competent, thoughtful, and deliberate, but aware of the expectations placed upon him, both within the force and in the communities he serves. Those expectations shift. At times they underestimate him. At other times they subject him to scrutiny. In either case, they shape the conditions under which he works.

Identity influences how the investigation unfolds. Ho is not defined solely by role or rank. Background, culture, and the assumptions of others affect how information is gathered and how it is offered. He moves between different social worlds, reading nuance in conversation, recognizing when behavior does not align with appearance, and interpreting how context shapes meaning. What remains unspoken often carries as much weight as what is said.

This produces a quieter form of detection. Ho does not rely on confrontation. He listens, observes, and allows situations to develop. Conversations matter. Context matters. Small shifts in behavior carry significance. A hesitation, a deflection, a choice of words, each contributes to the larger picture. People reveal more when they do not feel challenged. He allows this type of space to exist.

His position also alters how others respond. In some situations, he is treated as an outsider. In others, he is granted access precisely because he is perceived differently. His duality becomes a working advantage. He can move through environments where a more conventional officer might draw resistance, while also recognizing when he is being misread or underestimated. Both conditions provide information.

The series explores the tension between individuality and institution. Ho works within a system with established expectations and limitations. Procedure guides the investigation, yet flexibility is often required to navigate the realities of the environments he encounters. He is part of the police, but not entirely representative of its traditions. This distinction requires judgment. It also demands resilience. The work involves not only solving cases, but maintaining credibility where it is not automatically granted.

London provides the broader context. The city appears not as a single environment, but as a collection of overlapping communities, each with its own structure, assumptions, and codes of behavior. Crime develops within those layers, shaped by migration, economics, and shifting social identities. Reading those conditions becomes part of the investigative process. Ho reads the city through its people, recognizing how background and circumstance influence both action and motive.

Perspective becomes the central tool. The investigation depends on how the detective interprets what he sees, and how he perceives the position from which he is seeing it. Distance does not separate him from the case. It provides clarity. He recognizes assumptions others accept without question and tests them against what is actually present.

This approach carries its own challenges. Standing outside expectation can mean limited support, increased scrutiny, and the need to establish authority repeatedly. Progress is not always straightforward. Each decision may be examined more closely. Each action may require justification. The advantage of perspective comes with the cost of separation.

Even so, separation remains the source of the perspective's effectiveness. It allows movement between different worlds, the ability to question what appears settled, and the freedom to interpret the case from more than one position. The investigation develops through recognizing not only the crime, but the environment in which it occurs and the assumptions surrounding it.

The Chinese Detective shows perception is shaped by position. What the detective sees depends on where he stands, and how he is seen by others. Insight comes not from distance alone, but from the ability to use it.

THE TRAVELLING MAN—THE DRIFTER'S EYE

Movement defines *The Travelling Man*. The investigation begins without a fixed point, without a station, without a place to return to. Each location presents a new set of circumstances, a new group of people, and a problem to be understood quickly, often before it fully reveals itself. Detection unfolds in transit, shaped by observation rather than familiarity.

Played by Leigh Lawson, the central figure is not a police officer, nor a conventional detective. He is a professional gambler, a man whose livelihood depends on reading people, judging risk, and recognizing patterns under pressure. Those abilities transfer directly into investigation. He notices hesitation, overconfidence, and inconsistency. He recognizes when something does not align, even before the reason becomes clear.

There is no fixed structure supporting the work. No station. No department. No established authority. Each case emerges from circumstance, often by chance, sometimes through necessity. A situation presents itself, and involvement follows not from obligation, but from recognition. Something does not fit, and he chooses to follow it.

This produces a distinct investigative rhythm. There is no time to build a formal case, no access to official records, and no guarantee of cooperation. Information is gathered through conversation, observation, and brief encounters. A remark made in passing, a gesture offered without thought, a reaction arriving too quickly, each becomes part of the process. Conclusions develop through pattern recognition rather than accumulation.

Speed matters, but not in the conventional sense. The importance lies in how quickly a situation can be made clear, not how quickly action can be taken. Without the ability to return later, each moment carries weight. A missed detail may not present itself again. Decisions must be made with incomplete information, guided by instinct shaped through experience rather than procedure.

Freedom defines the role. He has no procedural limits, no jurisdictional boundaries, no requirement to justify each step. Questions can be asked without formal consequence. Movement is unrestricted. This flexibility allows entry into environments where a more visible authority might encounter resistance. But it also removes protection. Without authority, answers cannot be compelled. Without support, judgment stands alone. Every choice carries immediate consequence.

Detachment follows naturally from this position. The travelling man does not remain with the outcome. Once a situation resolves, he moves on. There is no report, no follow-up, no accumulation tied to a single place. Each investigation exists as a moment rather than part of an ongoing record. Experience builds differently, not through continuity, but through repetition across varied environments.

This repetition produces its own form of explanation. Patterns emerge across distance. The same motives appear in different settings. Greed, fear, ambition, deception, these do not belong to one place. They recur wherever people gather. Movement allows these connections to become visible. Without attachment to a single environment, comparison becomes broader, less influenced by familiarity or expectation.

The environments themselves shape the work. Casinos, hotels, transport hubs, and temporary spaces replace the fixed settings of other investigations. These are locations defined by transition, where identities are less stable and relationships more fluid. Information is harder to verify. Trust is provisional. The detective must rely on immediate perception rather than established knowledge.

This approach also carries limits. Depth is sacrificed for breadth. Without long-term presence, subtle relationships may remain hidden. Context may be incomplete. The absence of institutional support restricts what can be confirmed or enforced. The detective must recognize enough, quickly enough, to act before the opportunity passes.

Even so, the advantage remains clear. Movement prevents complacency. Each situation is approached without assumption. Familiar patterns appear in unfamiliar settings, allowing recognition without distraction. The detective sees connections others might overlook, not because they are inattentive, but because they are too close to their own environment.

The Travelling Man presents detection as a process shaped by motion. Cognizance comes from entering, observing, and leaving, carrying insight without attachment. The investigation does not settle. It passes through, leaving resolution behind and continuing forward.

The Travelling Man demonstrates the work may depend not on where a detective stands, but on the ability to see clearly while passing through.

DEATH IN PARADISE—FISH-OUT-OF-WATER

Displacement sharpens perception. In *Death in Paradise*, *Beyond Paradise*, and *Return to Paradise*, detection begins from a position of difference. The detective does not fully belong to the environment, and his or her separation exposes what others accept without question. Comprehension develops through contrast.

On the fictional Caribbean island of Saint Marie, the pattern is first established. British detectives arrive carrying habits formed elsewhere, expecting order, speed, and structure. The island resists those expectations. Heat slows movement. Conversations extend. Time operates differently. Crime still follows a precise internal logic, but the environment shapes how it unfolds and how it is perceived. What appears ordinary within the setting may conceal the essential detail.

Detective Inspector Richard Poole, played by Ben Miller, defines this initial stage. Formal, precise, and uncomfortable, he refuses to adapt. He dresses for London, insists on structure, and treats each case as something to be contained and resolved. His resistance becomes an advantage. Because he does not accept the environment, he questions it. Assumptions others rely on become visible to him as potential flaws.

His successors adjust the balance between distance and adaptation. Detective Inspector Humphrey Goodman, played by Kris Marshall, relaxes the rigidity without abandoning clarity. He appears distracted, even disordered, yet connects details through association. Where Poole imposes order, Goodman allows patterns to form. Detective Inspector Jack Mooney, portrayed by Ardal O'Hanlon, moves further toward *seeing* the people within the setting. He listens, observes, and allows conversations to develop. Familiarity increases, though enough distance remains to preserve perspective. Detective Inspector Neville Parker, played by Ralf Little, returns to a more pronounced form of discomfort. His sensitivity to the environment forces constant re-evaluation, turning unease into method.

The structure holds across these variations. The detective stands apart from the setting, never fully absorbed into it. That separation produces clarity. Behavior shaped by environment becomes easier to read when viewed from outside its assumptions. Each case follows a puzzle design, often involving a limited group of suspects within a contained framework. The solution depends on identifying how the crime occurred and why. Explanation arrives through arrangement, placing each detail into relation until contradiction resolves.

Beyond Paradise alters the conditions without abandoning the method. Goodman leaves Saint Marie and settles in the coastal town of Shipton Abbott. Movement gives way to continuity. The detective no longer passes through. He remains. Familiarity replaces immediate contrast. Repeated observation is developed through empathy rather than first encounters.

This shift changes the rhythm of the work. Cases unfold within a community in which the detective becomes a part and where relationships extend beyond a single investigation. Conversations carry history. Decisions carry consequence. The work no longer exists in isolation. It intersects with personal life, particularly through Goodman's relationship with Martha Lloyd, played by Sally Bretton. The problem is no longer how to interpret a place quickly, but how to maintain clarity while becoming connected to it.

Distance does not disappear. It changes form. The detective remains distinct in method, yet no longer stands entirely outside the environment. Insight develops through familiarity, through recognizing patterns over time. The puzzle structure remains intact, but the path to its solution emerges through accumulated knowledge rather than immediate contrast.

Return to Paradise reframes the same dynamic once more. Set in coastal Australia, the series introduces Detective Inspector Mackenzie Clarke, played by Anna Samson. She returns to a place she once knew, carrying memory, history, and unresolved relationships. The position shifts again. She is neither fully outsider nor fully insider.

This duality complicates perception. Prior knowledge provides context, yet also introduces assumption. The challenge lies in separating what is known from what is present. Familiarity can clarify, but it can also distort. Clarke must continually reassess her own perspective, determining when memory informs judgment and when it interferes with it.

The environment reinforces this tension. The Australian coastal setting expands physical space while maintaining social containment. Communities remain defined, yet shaped by distance and isolation. Relationships carry weight across time. Crime emerges from those conditions, requiring the detective to account for both immediate circumstance and prior connection.

Across all three series, the same investigative structure persists. Each case functions as a puzzle. Each solution depends on identifying the element which does not fit. What changes is the position from which the detective observes. Arrival produces clarity through difference. Settlement produces clarity through continuity. Return produces clarity through comparison between past and present.

Perspective becomes the determining factor. The method does not rely solely on evidence or procedure, but on how the detective interprets the environment in which the crime occurs. The same setting can conceal or reveal, depending on where the observer stands.

These variations demonstrate how detection adapts without losing form. The framework remains stable, but its application shifts with circumstance. The detective does not simply solve the case. The detective defines how the case is seen.

Together, these series show perception depends not only on what is observed, but on position. Distance, familiarity, and memory each provide a different kind of clarity. The solution emerges when those perspectives are brought into alignment.

MACDONALD & DODDS—THE UNEQUAL MIND

Contrast drives *McDonald & Dodds*. The investigation does not proceed from a single line of thought, but from the friction between two approaches which do not naturally align. Each detective sees the case differently. Clarity emerges when those differences begin to intersect.

Detective Chief Inspector Lauren MacDonald, played by Tala Gouveia, arrives in Bath with urgency and direction. She is direct, ambitious, and accustomed to movement. Her instinct is to act, to question, to impose structure. She expects progress to follow effort, and she presses the investigation forward, often before its shape has fully formed.

Detective Sergeant Dodds, portrayed by Jason Watkins, operates at a different pace. Quiet, observant, and methodical, he absorbs information rather than drives it. Details accumulate. Patterns take time. He notices what others pass over, not through force, but through attention. Where MacDonald moves outward, Dodds works inward, assembling the case piece by piece until coherence appears.

The difference between them is not reduced or resolved. It remains active. MacDonald creates momentum. Dodds creates interpretation. The investigation advances through the tension between those modes, not through their convergence into a single method. Each approach exposes the limits of the other. Action without reflection risks error. Reflection without action risks delay. The case develops in the space between.

Bath reinforces this dynamic. The city presents order, symmetry, and surface coherence, yet beneath its structure lies complexity, contradiction, and concealed motive. Appearances suggest clarity. Closer examination reveals disruption. The setting mirrors the partnership—one element defined by structure and presentation, the other by depth and interpretation.

The investigative rhythm follows this pattern. Early stages are driven by movement, interviews, leads, and rapid collection of information. Momentum builds. As the case develops, attention shifts. Details return. Statements are reconsidered. What seemed complete begins to fracture. Dodds' influence becomes more pronounced at this stage, not by taking control, but by redirecting focus. The solution emerges through re-examination, through recognizing what has already been seen but in a different way.

Authority operates differently within this structure. MacDonald holds rank, responsibility, and visible control. Decisions pass through her. The direction of the case depends on her judgment. Dodds holds none of the formal authority, yet shapes the investigation through insight. His influence is indirect but decisive. He does not lead in a conventional sense, yet without his contribution the case remains incomplete.

Their partnership does not follow the expected arc of opposition leading to similarity. They do not become versions of one another. The contrast persists, and persistence allows the method to function. Each continues to approach the work from a distinct position, and the value lies in the interaction between those positions rather than in any form of resolution.

The cases themselves reflect this structure. They appear straightforward, then reveal additional layers requiring reinterpretation. Initial assumptions prove incomplete. Motives shift. Connections emerge where none were first apparent. The investigation depends on the ability to hold multiple perspectives at once, to allow contradiction to exist long enough for meaning to develop.

This approach highlights a different aspect of detection. The work does not always depend on a singular insight or a dominant perspective. It can depend on the interaction between competing interpretations. One perspective challenges another. One fills gaps the other leaves. Appreciation forms through exchange rather than certainty.

The partnership becomes the method. Not a compromise, not a blending, but a sustained interaction where difference remains intact. Each detective contributes something essential, and the case advances only when both forms of thinking are allowed to operate.

McDonald & Dodds shows clarity can emerge from contrast. The solution does not belong to one mind alone. It develops through the space between them, where opposing approaches meet and reveal what neither could see independently.

PATIENCE—THE QUIET MIND

In *Patience*, investigation begins far from the front line, deep within departmental archives where closed cases sit in ordered silence. Patience Evans is a high-functioning neurodivergent, and her cognition shapes every step. She is introduced cataloguing and preserving records others have long since abandoned. No badge. No rank. No expectation of fieldwork. Her environment favors order, repetition, and control, conditions allowing information to be held long enough for structure to emerge—conditions aligned with her mental framework and the pressures she manages.

Her move into active cases comes through recognition rather than design. A detail held longer than others would allow. A pattern maintained without forcing resolution. A connection formed outside expected lines. Detective Bea Metcalf identifies value in this difference and brings Patience into the process, not as support, but as counterweight to established method. The premise settles quickly. Detection does not belong to a single mode of thought.

Patience works without authority or display. No reliance on pressure, no instinct for confrontation. Attention drives the work. Detail is retained, ordered, and revisited. Information is not skimmed for speed or ranked for immediate use. It is held until relationships surface. Language forms only one layer. Tone, timing, hesitation, omission carry equal weight. A pause may signal more than a statement. A deviation from expected behavior draws focus faster than any direct clue. A different rhythm takes hold. Progress remains internal until structure settles into place. Patterns align. Once coherence appears, movement follows. Until then, little registers from the outside.

The distinction matters because policing depends on urgency. Leads must be pursued, decisions made, pressure applied. Momentum can obscure quieter signals and force premature conclusions. Patience introduces restraint. Uncertainty is held rather than collapsed. Ambiguity is examined instead of reduced. When resolution arrives, it fits cleanly, each element in place without strain.

Friction develops alongside this advantage. Misunderstanding of neurodivergence persists within the workplace. Difference is often treated as deficit rather than variation. Expectations lean toward conformity with neurotypical norms, creating pressure to adjust rather than adapt the system itself. Patience does not conform. Her process resists compression into conventional tempo, and conflict follows.

The method also produces practical advantages. Interviews conducted without pressure allow subjects to settle into natural cadence. Speech aligns with behavior. Discrepancies surface through delivery rather than contradiction. The gap between statement and intent becomes visible. Experienced interrogators recognize this effect, though few sustain it with such consistency.

Limits remain. Patience holds no authority to compel response or accelerate inquiry. Progress depends on access, time, and cooperation. Sensory overload presents another challenge. Noise, unpredictability, or excessive input can fracture focus. Withdrawal becomes necessary, not avoidance, but recalibration. Work pauses until equilibrium returns.

The greater obstacle often lies with others. Neurodivergence falls outside conventional expectations of competence within policing. Silence is read as disengagement. Precision goes unnoticed because it lacks overt confidence. Credibility must be established through outcome rather than presentation.

The series avoids exaggeration. No savant shorthand. No imposed brilliance. Patience remains specific, her strengths and limits in balance. Contribution comes from how information is processed, not from spectacle.

Set against *Astrid et Raphaëlle*, the French-Belgian original from which it draws its premise, *Patience* refines rather than replicates. The core dynamic remains—a neurodivergent civilian working alongside a police detective—but the British version shifts tone and emphasis. The partnership with Bea Metcalf develops through recognition, not friction. Trust builds through results rather than personality clash. Restraint replaces volatility. By removing overt drama, the series reinforces its central idea. Effective investigation often unfolds without display.

Here, the boundaries of investigative practice expand. Law enforcement depends on interpretation, and no single approach holds a monopoly on reaching it. Patience represents one of those approaches. Not faster. Not louder. More exact.

LUDWIG—THE PATTERN MIND

Detection in *Ludwig* begins with pattern. The problem is not approached as a sequence of events, but as a system to be decoded. What matters is not simply what happened, but how the elements relate, how they align, and where they fail to do so.

The central figure, John *Ludwig* Taylor, played by David Mitchell, enters the world of investigation from an entirely different discipline. A creator of puzzles, he works within systems built to be solved. Every element has purpose. Every solution exists within the structure of the problem. When drawn into a criminal investigation, he carries the same expectation with him. An answer exists, and it can be found if the structure is properly understood.

This perspective immediately sets him apart. He does not begin with interviews or procedure. He begins by looking for form. He studies the arrangement of events, the placement of individuals, the sequence of actions. He is less concerned with what people say than with how their accounts fit together. Inconsistency becomes the primary clue. Where others accept a statement at face value, he examines its position within the larger pattern.

The series pushes detection toward abstraction. The case is not simply a narrative to be reconstructed, but a configuration to be solved. Each piece of information carries weight only in relation to the others. A detail matters not because it is dramatic, but because it either supports or disrupts the structure being formed. The investigation becomes a process of testing alignment, adjusting the model until it holds.

This produces a distinctive investigative rhythm. Rather than moving steadily forward through interviews and evidence gathering, the process advances in stages of recognition. Periods of observation give way to moments of clarity, when the pattern resolves enough to suggest a new direction. Progress is not always visible from the outside. It occurs internally, as the detective refines his interpretation of the system he is attempting to map.

The series also makes clear the world of crime is not a puzzle constructed for neat resolution. Unlike the problems Ludwig is accustomed to creating, real events are shaped by chance, emotion, and imperfect decision-making. People do not behave according to design. They act impulsively, irrationally, and sometimes without clear motive. This creates friction between method and material.

That friction becomes central to the character. Ludwig must learn not every inconsistency is intentional, and not every pattern is complete. Some gaps cannot be filled. Some elements resist placement. The challenge shifts from imposing order to recognizing when order exists and when it must be adjusted to account for irregularity.

A notable distance defines his approach. He engages with the case at a conceptual level, focusing on coherence rather than emotional impact. This allows him to remain clear-headed, but also creates difficulty in situations requiring empathy or intuitive judgment. He fathoms systems more readily than people, and the investigation forces him to reconcile those two modes of thinking.

The series uses this tension effectively. Pattern provides the framework, but it cannot remain rigid. As new information emerges, the structure must change. The solution is not a fixed design waiting to be discovered, but a model evolving as appreciation deepens. The investigation becomes dynamic rather than static, shaped by the interaction between logic and reality.

Ludwig represents the pattern mind taken to its furthest point. Where Holmes observes and Poirot arranges, Ludwig constructs. He builds a representation of the case and tests it against the available evidence, refining it until it holds. The method emphasizes clarity, precision, and internal consistency.

Pattern alone is not enough. Structure can reveal truth only if it remains flexible. When it becomes too rigid, it risks excluding the very elements defining human behavior. The most effective solutions account for both order and disruption, logic and unpredictability.

The pattern mind reflects a particular discipline. It seeks clarity without oversimplification, structure without rigidity. Meaning is built piece by piece, as long as the design remains open to revision.

PROFESSOR T—THE FRACTURED MIND

Clarity, in *Professor T*, does not arrive through order or patience. It emerges under pressure. The mind solving the crime is also the mind complicating it. Thought is precise, but not always controlled. Insight is sharp, but accompanied by tension, contradiction, and strain.

At the center of the series is Professor Jasper Tempest, portrayed in the British adaptation by Ben Miller, a criminologist whose intellectual ability is matched by a complex and often fragile psychological state. His cognizance of criminal behavior is exceptional. He recognizes patterns, motives, and inconsistencies with a level of precision placing him ahead of those around him. Yet the same intensity creates difficulty. The world does not always conform to the order he expects, and when it does not, the response is not adjustment, but discomfort.

The series places the act of thinking itself under pressure. The investigation is not only about solving the crime. It is also about managing the conditions under which a solution becomes possible. The detective's mind is both instrument and obstacle. Insight must pass through anxiety, memory, and internal conflict before it can be expressed.

This tension extends across every version of the character. The series originates in Belgium, where Koen De Bouw first established the role, presenting a figure defined by intellectual brilliance and emotional complexity. The concept was later adapted in France and Germany, each version adjusting tone and emphasis while retaining the central idea of a criminologist whose mind operates at a different frequency. The British adaptation continues this progression, shaping the character within a more traditional detective framework while preserving the instability defining him.

Across these versions, details shift. Setting, style, and supporting characters change, but the essential dynamic remains. The detective is not fully aligned with the world he inhabits. Perception is sharper, but also more demanding. He requires order, yet is confronted constantly by disorder. The investigation becomes a negotiation between those conditions.

The process follows a distinct path. The professor does not simply gather information. He interprets it through an internal model shaped by experience and sensitivity. A crime scene is not just evidence. It is a configuration of behavior. Each action reflects intention, and each intention must be understood within a psychological framework. The solution depends on aligning these elements into a structure making sense both logically and behaviorally.

The series also emphasizes the cost of this approach. Clarity achieved through analysis is not stable. It must be maintained, often with difficulty. Social interaction becomes a challenge. Emotional responses are heightened. Effectiveness depends on managing these factors as much as on intellectual ability. The work is not only external. It is internal, and ongoing.

Dependence on others further complicates the method. The professor does not function easily within a police structure, yet relies on it to act on his conclusions. Authority and insight separate. He sees what has happened, but others must translate his conclusions into action. The result is a partnership between stability and instability, between structure and disruption.

Professor T represents the fractured mind—the idea of brilliance coexisting with vulnerability, and the qualities enabling affinity also make it more difficult to achieve. It places intellect under pressure, where clarity remains possible but never comes easily.

This approach reveals both strength and limitation. The mind can penetrate complexity with remarkable precision, but cannot always contain what it uncovers. The investigation becomes not only a search for truth, but a process of sustaining the ability to recognize it.

Insight is not a stable condition. It can be fleeting, difficult, and hard-won, emerging from a balance requiring constant maintenance. The solution is not simply found. It is achieved, and sometimes at a cost.

CASE SUMMARY

Throughout these series, the detective is no longer defined by role, rank, or position within a system. The investigation is shaped by the individual, by the way a particular mind observes, interprets, and perceives the world. This is not a departure from exploring the profession of investigation. Instead, it is an expansion of it. What emerges is not a single model of detection, but a range of approaches, each grounded in a different way of thinking.

The consulting detective observes with unusual precision. The methodical investigator imposes order, arranging facts until they reveal meaning. Another reads people, recognizing patterns of behavior repeating across time and circumstance. The specialist applies knowledge, turning objects into evidence. The outsider sees clearly because distance removes assumption. The drifter moves across environments, identifying patterns extending beyond any single place. Some work in contrast with others, their differences generating insight. Others rely on stillness, allowing meaning to emerge without force. Some approach crime as a structure to be solved. Others rely on a mind shaped by tension, contradiction, or instability.

These approaches clarify something essential. Detection is not defined by procedure alone. It is shaped by perception. The same set of facts can produce different conclusions depending on how they are understood. The distinction lies not in the evidence, but in the interpretation of it. The profession depends as much on how a detective thinks as on what a detective does.

This perspective reframes the role of the detective within the larger structure of the book. Earlier sections establish the system, the organization, and the evolution of the work. Here, the focus shifts to the individual as an operating element within the profession. The case becomes a point of contact between problem and perception, where outcome depends on how those two elements interact.

These portrayals do not replace the professional model. They exist alongside it, revealing another dimension of the same work. The police officer builds a case through procedure and persistence. The amateur or unconventional detective arrives at knowledge through insight, association, or interpretation. Both perform the same function. They reach it by different means.

Taken together, this section completes the framework established across the book. The system defines the work. The profession carries it out. The intellect shapes how it is understood. The modern era alters its conditions. The individual reveals the final element, detection as an act of thought.

Thought can take many forms. It may be structured or intuitive, controlled or unstable, grounded or detached. It may rely on knowledge, experience, or perspective. What remains constant is the task itself, to make sense of events, to find coherence in confusion, and to recognize truth within the available evidence.

The detective may operate within a system or outside it, may follow procedure or depart from it, but the function does not change. Investigation remains a profession defined not only by structure and method, but by the capacity to see clearly, think precisely, and understand what others cannot.

EPILOGUE—THE LAST WORD

The detective remains one of the most enduring figures in storytelling, not because of the crimes surrounding him, but because of the questions he represents. Something has happened. Something does not make sense. The task is to understand it.

On British television, the task assumes many forms, shaped by changing times, different environments, and the evolution of both crime and society. The essential problem has not changed. It is the problem of making sense of incomplete information.

Within the series considered here, the detective appears as part of a system, as a professional within an institution, as an intellect working outside it, and as an individual shaped by experience, personality, and circumstance. Each version offers a different approach to the same challenge. The intelligence officer gathers fragments and assembles a picture never fully confirmed. The working detective builds a case able to stand in court. The literary detective resolves a puzzle through logic and observation. The modern detective navigates a world of abundant information but limited certainty. The outsider approaches the problem from a position defined not by rules or procedure, but by perception.

No single approach is complete. Each reveals something about the nature of the work, but also its limitations. The system provides structure, but can restrict movement. Experience brings insight, but can also shape expectation. Intellect offers clarity, but can overlook the unpredictable nature of human behavior. Independence allows freedom, but removes support. The detective works within these tensions, balancing what is known against what can be proven, what is seen against what can be understood.

Over time, a central truth emerges. Detection is not simply a profession or a skill. It is a way of thinking. It is a calling. It requires the ability to hold uncertainty without resolving it too quickly, to recognize the first explanation is not always correct, and to continue working when the answer is not immediately apparent. It demands attention, patience, and a willingness to reconsider what has already been assumed.

In fiction, the process often appears cleaner than it is in reality. Clues align. Motives are revealed. The solution emerges at the right moment and is explained with clarity. The structure satisfies because it resolves uncertainty into lucidity. In practice, the work is rarely so complete. Information is missing. People do not behave predictably. Decisions are made without full knowledge. The truth, when found, is sometimes partial, sometimes ambiguous, and occasionally beyond reach.

The difference does not diminish the value of these stories. It explains their appeal. They present a version of the world in which confusion can be reduced to order, where the unknown can be made known, and where persistence leads to resolution. They reflect not only how investigations are conducted, but how they are understood, as processes driven by clarity, purpose, and the belief truth can be discovered through careful attention.

The best of these series acknowledge the cost. The detective carries the work beyond the case. The knowledge gained is not easily set aside. Experience accumulates, shaping how the next problem is approached. Over time, the job leaves its mark, not only in what has been solved, but in what has been seen and understood.

Here, the different versions of the detective converge. The intelligence officer, the police investigator, the consulting mind, and the outsider all face the same underlying challenge. They must decide what matters, what can be trusted, and what the available information means. They separate signal from noise, intention from coincidence, and truth from appearance. The methods differ, but the function remains consistent.

At a certain point, the distinction between professional and amateur loses importance. Authority provides access, resources, and structure, but does not guarantee intelligibility. Insight may come from experience, intellect, observation, or a way of seeing outside expectation. The ability to solve the problem depends less on position than on perception.

One idea persists across every version. The detective succeeds not because he knows everything, but because he knows what to look for. He recognizes the detail that does not fit, the answer that raises another question, the moment when the explanation fails. He returns to that point and examines it again, and again, until it yields.

This is the part of the work that does not change. Tools evolve. Methods develop. Technology expands what can be known and how quickly it can be accessed. The essential act remains the same. It is the act of paying attention, of thinking carefully, and of resisting the temptation to accept the obvious answer when something about it feels wrong.

The enduring power of the detective lies in that resistance. It is the refusal to let uncertainty remain unresolved, balanced by the knowledge certainty is not always possible. It is the willingness to continue, even when the path is unclear, and to recognize the solution, if it comes, will come through effort rather than assumption.

In the end, the detective does not restore order so much as reveal it, or reveal the absence of it. The work is not about imposing meaning on events, but about discovering meaning already present, however difficult it may be to see.

That is the last word on the detective. Not the method. Not the system. Not the structure. The act itself. To look closely. To think clearly. To understand what happened, and why. And then to move on to the next question.

ABOUT THE AUTHOR

Paul Bishop is a retired Los Angeles Police Department detective with a thirty-five-year career, including more than two decades specializing in the investigation of sexualized assaults. He later supervised a unit of thirty detectives and became a nationally recognized instructor in interview and interrogation techniques, teaching law enforcement agencies across the United States.

He is the author of fifteen novels and four nonfiction works, including the award-winning *Lie Catchers*. His writing spans crime fiction, Westerns, and studies of investigative practice across literature, film, and television.

Bishop is the co-creator and co-host of the Six-Gun Justice Podcast and has written for both television and film. He lives in Southern California.

www.ingramcontent.com/pod-product-compliance
Lightning Source LLC
LaVergne TN
LVHW020710110826
845149LV00012B/2195

* 9 7 9 8 9 9 5 3 5 7 1 4 8 *